I0790499

AuthorHouse™
1663 Liberty Drive
Bloomington, IN 47403
www.authorhouse.com
Phone: 833-262-8899

Published by AuthorHouse 09/30/2020

ISBN: 978-1-6655-0182-8 (sc)
ISBN: 978-1-6655-0181-1 (e)

Print information available on the last page.

I DRINK MY MOO
I DO MY POO
THAT'S ALL I DO

One Humans Journey Through Life

ROBERT BAKER

authorHOUSE®

Mom, Dad and Bundle of Joy – Bobby 1939

Contents

My special thanks to my cousin "Jeff Hatton" who was a good friend and teacher in the development of this book. I'm not a "techi" person and at my age it's not easy to tackle computer complexities.

Jeff was kind enough to teach me how to develop this book on the computer i.e., insert pictures, make whole scale changes, taught me how to use Office Writer functions and even took the time to proofread. He did all this in a way that made it easy for me.

I want to personally thank my parents for making my life possible and I want to give a special thanks to my kids for making my life necessary.

I'm thankful for the times I've had in this lifetime and for the people who have crossed my path. Everyone has played a role in the development of this human being. Everyone has made me the person I am today, good or bad. This includes grandparents, parents, aunts and uncles, sister, cousins, wives, children and even sons-in-law and grandchildren. Now I've even got great-grandchildren. What a cast.

Introduction

Have you ever wondered what kind of footprint you would leave on this earth? Who would look at it and know what it was, who it was, or what it did when it was put here? I haven't done anything special or heroic but what I did do is exactly that..... "What I did". This writing is not a footprint, but a word picture of me and intended to just be that. My past or upbringing might have molded someone or put a thought in someone's mind that resonates today, but it's probably by accident, if that's actually what happened.

When all is said and done, my life boils down to "what have I said" and "what I have done". Have I said the right things at the right time and have I done the right things at the right time? Pretty Profound.

I have always thought I would be an inspiration to the family members that followed me. At least I have always hoped I would. But as I am getting older, I believe the following generations are actually an inspiration to me. I hope this helps me in my old age as I have always thought, just maybe something of me might help the younger generations in their lives.

When I think of the direction the world is heading and how much different my kids and Grandkids are with their values of life, as opposed to mine, I thought I might want to write down thoughts from my childhood and growing up years. I guess that includes all the way up to where I am now. (By the way, I'm still growing.) These thoughts are not meant to change the world or even try to change the way my kids and Grandkids think, but they are what molded me as to who I am and what makes me tick today. I also think a lot of these thoughts are similar with most of my generation. There is a lot of changing going on.

You constantly hear from the older generation (I'm one), **"I'm sure glad I am as old as I am and I wouldn't want to be the age of my Grandkids"**. With values being so different today, I really do mean it. I'm sure that youngsters get tired hearing this from us, but they have to put up with it. At least as long as we're here.

Why would a person want to write something like this? I'm sure there are things within these pages I have done that will offend and possibly bring back memories. Some things may not be enjoyable to one person or another. But they are moments that appeared in my life and some might be able to learn from it, or get a chuckle. Time seems like an eternity when you are in your 20's and 30's. When you find your way into your 70's, you just might start reading obituary columns, and seeing that people are dying at your age or even younger. It starts to sink in you just might not be here too much longer. When I was in my 20's I never thought people grew old, I thought they were just old. Someone must have put them here like that for us. However, we actually pass through this life for a very short period of time and as we get older, we find out it's faster than you think or want it to be.

As I said, this writing might offend some, but the reader has to remember when we grew up, times were different. We've been through wars, conflicts, good and bad Presidents, and good and bad economy. The time of this writing is the most critical than any I can remember. The economy just started getting better and we get hit with a Pandemic and now I'm worried about where it's going. This bothers me because this means my kids. Grandkids, and grandchildren are going to have to pay for it. (This is not intended to be political, but congress has progressed to a point where they aren't even thinking of us Americans, only of themselves.) Growing up, we didn't even know we were going through these good or bad phases, but we did. After all, when you're young, you're invincible.

By my writing this, it doesn't mean I'm right any more than the youngsters of today are right. It just means at some point in history, this is the way I thought it to be. It's not intended to offend, and the reader might be able to understand a little more of our generation or more specifically, (my) thoughts.

I'm not from the smartest of the generations (I think our forefathers were the smartest as they had to write the constitution and write it so we would be able to live it for years to come). We were smart enough to learn from each other and I believe we prepared a better place for the following generations. Sometimes we come across as "this is the only way" to do something, but actually we just might be giving the listener something to start with or just another point of view. Whatever it is, my hope is that this writing gives you something to think about.

Thought I'd put something together for you to think about. It sums up how we deal with growing older. You see, we grew up learning from our parents and our peers, and were involved in some big decisions during life (school, kids, buying material things like homes, working, moving, etc.). During these periods we were looked upon as being pretty smart. At least that's the way I think we were viewed. Now we're getting older, and it seems we're not looked upon in a similar way. Today our youngsters don't think we know anything at all. It makes one feel like we're being put out to pasture.

A Poem to Y'all	**My mood is bad – can you tell?**
I cannot see	My bodies drooping
I cannot pee	Have trouble pooping
I cannot chew	The Golden Years
I cannot screw	Have come at last

Oh my God, what can I do?   The Golden Years Can Kiss

"My Ass"

> My memory shrinks
> My hearing stinks
> No sense of smell
> I look like hell

Youngsters today don't have to put up with the everyday life things that we had at our age. Things that change are balance, vocabulary, and thought process. I used to be able to run up a ladder to high places, always have the correct words at the tip of my tongue, and think about things in the proper order. Now I sometimes bump into walls, stagger down the hall and get lightheaded when I stand up. I have a hard time thinking of the correct word to say and this frustrates me and it seems like I definitely can't get from "A" to "Z" in the correct order. Doctors tell us this is normal.

I remember growing up and thinking the most important things I had to do was to get through the day enjoying myself. Of course when I was young that meant my chores had to be done or at least I had to be able to pass them off as being done. Later on, the biggest problems I had was whether or not my paycheck was going to cover our expenses, which expenses were important to our family, where was my future going, etc. Now I worry about things like;

"If I get down on my knees, will I be able to get up",
"When I pee, am I ever going to get done",
"How many times am I going to get up during the night",
"Did I take my pills like I was supposed to today",
"Why isn't that TV show on tonight like it's supposed to be",
"Are we running out of toilet paper", (big item during pandemic)
"What was that person's name",
"When I stand at the bottom of a flight of stairs, did I just come down or am I going up",

"What am I forgetting".

These things now take a lot of my time. They used to be just bumps in my early days.

The year of this writing starts in 2009 and probably is finished sometime in 2020. Do you realize the ones who are just starting college this fall were born in 2002? The following are just some of the things they don't remember:

(1) They are too young to remember the space shuttle blowing up.
(2) Their lifetime has always included AIDS.
(3) The CD was introduced fourteen years before they were born.
(4) They have always had CABLE.
(5) Jay Leno was the big star on the Tonight Show, but was recently replaced.
(6) Popcorn has always been microwaved.
(7) They never took a swim and thought about Jaws.
(8) They don't know who Mork was or where he was from.
(9) They never heard: "Where's the Beef?", "I'd walk a mile for a Camel", or "De Plane, Boss, De Plane".
(10) McDonald's never came in Styrofoam containers.
(11) They don't have a clue how to use a typewriter.

Setting the Stage — Prior to Me

Some Early History:

I was born January 15, 1939, which at that time was NOT Martin Luther King's celebrated birthday. I admit he was a very important person in history, but my birthday is mine and I don't share very well. I always liked my birthday being January 15th because I just went through Christmas and boom.....here comes my birthday and that means one thing—more presents. I automatically started counting the days (21) from Christmas to the big day. I think that's why birthdays and Christmas' were always big in the Baker family.

I gave my daughters a teddy bear made with the remnants of their Great-Grandmother Baker's mink coat and told the story of that coat in rhyme. While that is something we can grab onto as part of our history, it took a lot of people to get me here for the short time I'll spend on this earth. These are the things I remember being told and some I learned after the fact:

The Bakers are related to Sir Isaac Newton. (I borrowed his bio.) He was born in 1642 and died in 1727. He was a mathematician and physicist, one of the foremost scientific intellects of all time. He was born in Woolsthorpe, near Grantham in Lincolnshire. He entered Cambridge University in 1661. Boy that was a long time ago. I have a letter dated January 1922, and sent to Grandma Baker identifying this information. The letter continues to state that Sir Isaac Newton's family married into the "Estes" family who later married into the Bakers.

The Estes family were tobacco farmers in the south, and they owned slaves for farming their property. Of course they were sensitive to the South's cause during the civil war as it was going to be an economic hardship on farm owners if all of a sudden they didn't have workers. And true to a lot of farmers in the south, the Estes family lost everything after the civil war because they now couldn't pay their taxes. The letter was sent from a Baker relative (living in

Nampa, Oregon at the time), and identified some of our early history and included this information. The letter further states the Estes family had a lot of artifacts handed down from Sir Isaac Newton's estate. Note: Sir Isaac Newton never married and didn't have many immediate heirs to pass things on to. As a result of their tax problem, the Estes family lost all the artifacts they owned from Sir Isaac Newton.

According to the January 1922 letter the Bakers married into the Estes family and were given a couple of slaves as a wedding present. This was the custom in those days and the slaves were part of her dowry given by her parents, (a dowry is what a woman brings with her into marriage). The Bakers didn't believe in slavery and deeded 10 acres of their land to one of the slaves, a woman. I believe the woman slave later became a "wet nurse" (one who breast feeds others baby's). I don't know what happened to the other slave as the letter didn't write anything further about that person.

I was told that Estes Park, Colorado was named for a member of the Estes family who was a miner where the park is. Don't know much more about him than that, but it sounds good. Jason Newton Baker (who married Louise Blay Estes) drove the first stagecoach from St. Joseph, Missouri, up Pikes Peak, Colorado. Jason Newton Baker was born in England prior to coming to America. In those days it was a pretty good feat.

I have a pistol (E .R. Johnson firearms/cycle company, 32 caliber 5 shot) passed on to me as a pistol carried by one of my great uncles as a shoulder pistol when he played poker. I have tried to find out anything about that pistol that could be interesting to our family, (pistol has a serial number 458163) but since the Johnson firearms company went out of business in 1930, there are no records. We also had a relative who was a "horse thief" in the early days of our family, but don't have anything to back that up.

My great-grandparents (James Daniel & Anna Amos) "Huntsinger" migrated to Kansas in a covered wagon (just like the movies) and ended up in Mankato, Kansas area owning a section of land they acquired in a land rush. **Note: A land rush is when the government designates an area of land to be given to local residents.** The west was populated by enticing residents from back east to move out west by offering free land. This is why the Huntsingers moved to Kansas from Ohio.

**My Great Grandma
Anna Amos Huntsinger**

I wonder what a covered wagon trip would be like from Ohio to Kansas?

To participate in a land rush farmers would line up on horseback and buggies and race to a portion of land they wanted. Hence, land rush. There usually were fights and some shady deals made resulting from these races. Great Granddad Huntsinger acquired his section of land this way. (A section of land is 640 acres but each farmer got one fourth of that….160 acres.)

As I have stated., my Great Grandparents came to Kansas in a covered wagon and stayed with my great-grandfather's brother. Just like families of today, the brother's wives couldn't get along and the brother's wife told my great-grandfather they had to move.

Having no where to move, my great-grandfather noticed there was a deep dry creek that ran through their newly acquired property and my great-grandfather dug a cave (room) into the side of the creek. He covered the entrance with a blanket. This was their home for a month while he was building their "sod house". **A sod house is normally built using "slices" of prairie grass 18" X 36".** These slices are layered onto each other which become the walls of the home. The walls end up being 3 feet thick which was cool in the summer and warm in the winter. This is what the doctor ordered in those days as there wasn't any air-conditioning and heat was usually a fireplace which doubled as a cook stove. The inside walls were plastered to remove the dirt look on the inside. The sod houses were usually a one room house. A hole (root cellar) was dug in the floor to store food which became the first "refrigerators". Aren't we glad improvements have been made?

They later built a wood frame home attached to the sod house and eventually the home became a two story (due to the fact they had 8 kids) later in years. The sod house portion became the cook house because of the thickness of the walls and when it's usefulness was no more, it was torn down.

Just think about it…...Those of you grandkids who have babies, are of a same generation "difference" to me that I am to the people I'm writing about. From that you can see the many changes in life today.

Grandma Baker (**Keturah**, named for the 2nd wife of Abraham who bore him six sons as stated in the 25th chapter of Genesis in the Bible), we called her Kitty, graduated from high school and was actually on the school's "all girl" basketball team. That's right; they had an all girl basketball team back then. Uniforms were different.

A lot of youngsters didn't complete school in those days, but the Huntsinger kids all finished high school and most went to college and became lawyers. In those days you didn't need a college degree to teach school and Grandma Baker taught school for a couple of years after graduating high school. She actually taught school in "The

Little Red Schoolhouse" currently located at Knott's Berry Farm, in Los Angeles, California.

I went to the internet and looked up the history on the Little Red Schoolhouse and the write-up said the schoolhouse is still located in Beloit, Kansas on Hwy #24. However, I know for fact the original schoolhouse was moved to Knott's Berry Farm in California and is still there today. Knotts Berry Farm even changed some of the features of the actual school. Beloit citizens built a replacement schoolhouse (which is an exact duplicate to the original one) and placed it on Hwy #24. Still there today and you can go through it.

This is the "Little Red Schoolhouse" Grandma Baker taught school for two years

In the days of the one room schoolhouse, students were expected to learn from each other, were self-reliant and worked quietly. Children would sing the multiplication tables by singing them on the playground to songs like "Yankee Doodle". Teachers were leaders in the community. At the time that Grandma Huntsinger Baker was in school, a teacher's salary was between $10–40 per month. Her salary was $40.00 per month. Many were expected to be single and remain so as long as they were teachers.

There is a "memorial to the Huntsingers" located on Hwy #24 just outside Mankato in a roadside park. It's a tribute to the Huntsingers as original settlers of the area. I have taken my girls there when they were smaller and Donna and Bryan have both been there. Bryan was only nine months old at the time and I'm sure he doesn't remember anything about it.

Granddad Roy Baker never went past the 4th grade. He was one of 5 children in a farmer's family (moved from Missouri to Lebanon, Kansas area). His mother had died during child birth and his father couldn't raise a family and perform farm chores, so he "farmed" out 4 of his kids (and kept Granddad Roy to work on the farm as he was the oldest son). As I was told, his father (my great granddad), **Oscar Eugene Baker**, did not allow any of his kids to be adopted. Granddad Roy had three sisters and one brother. One of the sisters went to a family and the father of the family became the Governor of the State of Kansas. His name was Willis Joshua Bailey, who was a Republican and served as Governor from 1903 to 1905. That sister was able to go to college, and, while attending, met and married John Brookens' dad (who became a circuit judge). The Baker boys became cattle ranchers, farmers, and Granddad Roy eventually became a barber.

Grandma Keturah (Kitty) and Granddad Roy Claude were married January 5, 1910 and moved to Beloit in 1913. That's a long time ago.

I had a completely different account of the Baker history until Grandma Baker's 100th birthday. I had always thought (don't know where the information came from) that Granddad Baker was an only child and his mother had died during childbirth and his father married a lady with 4 kids. So, I never pursued any information about the other kids as it didn't seem important at the time. Well, I was wrong. Some of you will remember when we all went to Beloit, Kansas (Hilltop Nursing home) to celebrate Grandma Bakers 100th birthday. Anyway, I remember when I went in, I was told to go over to a table and meet John Brookens. He was the son of Granddad Roy Bakers sister (whose foster father was Governor Bailey) and he had knowledge of the Baker clan. That's when I learned the above story about the Baker kids. John Brookens was a cousin to my dad and when we talked, I did learn information about the Bakers and my dad that I didn't know.

Granddad Roy went on to become Beloit, Kansas' town judge, city council member, owned a barber and beauty shop, 3 apartment buildings and shaved patients at the local hospital on Mondays. Monday was the day of the week that barbers had off (in addition to Sunday's). Granddad Baker would also buy an old home every year and fix it up and sell it for profit. Good work ethics in those days.

My Granddad Roy Baker.

Looks very successful for a man who only went through the 4th grade. Wish I had his smarts.

Farmer as a young man, barber, city councilman, town Judge, successful businessman.

Grandma Kitty Baker played the organ in church for forty years and was a concert pianist. She played at church for so long, she had her own parking space. The pastor didn't even have one. As a youngster she had only 12 lessons and actually taught herself how to play. She played at weddings and funerals and taught piano and voice lessons to locals until the later years of her life. She said in a Grandma Book to me that she had perfect pitch. She was also musician of the year for the state of Kansas on two different occasions. Imagine, all this with only 12 lessons. Very talented.

Don't know much about the history of my mom's parents. I was always told Grandma Bowen (maiden name Maupin) was a quarter Cherokee Indian. Her mother would have been half Cherokee which was not cool in those days. Early history called some of these people "half breeds" and they were looked down on. That makes my mom an eighth and I am a 16th Cherokee. I look upon that as a compliment.

People don't realize today that "racial" issues have been around forever. The races are just different from time to time. I remember being told when my dad grew up in Beloit, Kansas, there weren't any "black" people living in town. So, who did they have to fight and degrade, i.e., the Catholics. Yep, they constantly fought between the two religions. So, I guess what I get from this is that we will always find something to fight about with our neighbors.

BOMB SHELL - Darbie and I both had our DNA's tested and recently found neither of us has any American Indian blood in our bodies. Darbie had always been told she had American Indian blood in her history also. So, none of you have any American Indian blood unless you got it from the other side of the family tree. However, Ancestry.com also told us that even though something doesn't show up in the DNA, it is possible for generations to miss or bypass some of the DNA. This is due to the fact that children only inherit 25% from each parent. Interesting. But I find it hard to believe this would be missed in all the generations.

I don't know if Grandma Bowen graduated high school and I don't really know if Granddad Bowen did either. He appears to be intelligent due to his handwriting skills when he wrote his World War I diary and he did work in the Library at Ft. Leavenworth, Kansas after his army career. I did publish his diary of his time in WWI, under the title **"Getting To Know Granddad"**. It's still for sale at Barnes and Noble and Amazon.com. (I'm not marketing.) This book lets you know a little about Granddad Bowen at a certain time in his life as well as how WWI was fought. He died at age 67 from Tuberculosis and Grandma Bowen died (I believe) around 93 thinking she owned Australia. I have a lot of fond memories while visiting their home on 203 Elm Street, Leavenworth, Kansas from when I was a little boy. Good times with my cousins were had at that home. I do know that Granddad Bowen came from the Pittsburgh, Pennsylvania area.

The reason I published his diary was that when I read it, I actually did get to know my Granddad Bowen. Since I was 10 when he died, I really didn't remember much about him or why he was the way he was. I'm not saying he was anything different, but he was a retired Army First Sergeant. Granddad's was a place where us cousins would meet and play in the garage or on the lawn. At that age, I was always afraid of him. (He already was retired and had over 30 years in the military.) As a result, he was gruff and that frightened me. He kept by himself and didn't interchange much with us grandkids. At least not much with me. Jo Ann and I were the only ones that lived away from Leavenworth, Kansas so we didn't interface with Granddad Bowen except when we visited. He was a saxophone player who played in the 7th Calvary band at Fort Leavenworth and later worked in the Book Store at Fort Leavenworth.

Their home on 203 Elm Street, Leavenworth, Kansas is registered on the "National Historical" society list. The last time I was through the home was about 1995. Darbie and I happened to be driving down Elm Street (I was showing her the old home) and they were having a tour of historical homes in Leavenworth. We stopped our car and I got to give Darbie a tour. It was sure small, but it brought back a bunch of memories. I had always remembered it as being very large. I would hope that my grandkids would have some memories of my homes and being there at different times. (I remember Lacy telling me she always remembered the "French" telephone I had in the bedroom and she would always play with it.)

One of the great times I have in my later years is that whenever I pass through Leavenworth, Kansas on a trip to or from somewhere, the cousins who are left, usually get together at my cousin Jill's farm. To me it's probably liken to a school reunion, i.e., we are older and we sit around and have a cool one and tell stories and probably a lie or two. Most of us are retired but some of the kids are still paying into SOC so we can continue our retirement. (Sometimes I think that's why we have kids.)

My mom was born in Wichita Falls, Texas. She was an army brat. Since Granddad Bowen was stationed at Fort Leavenworth for 18 years of his military career, mom pretty much grew up in Leavenworth, Kansas. I think she was a popular girl and early pictures show her to be pretty. She didn't finish high school but I think she went into her senior year.

Mom and Dad with that cute Little "Bundle of Joy in 1939

Mom had a photographic memory which helped her when she went to work at Boeing. I used to test her with Life Magazine's ads. She would look at the magazine and I would ask her where the ads were in the magazine. She got most right. Later when she went to work at Boeing (she was hired when Boeing was changing from telephone operators to dial phones) they put her in Central Files and had all the executive's correspondence go across her desk. She later became a supervisor of that department and was one of the first two female supervisors at Boeing.

She was married before my dad for only about six months, (I don't know his name and her divorce was due to physical abuse). She met my dad at Fort Leavenworth Army Base (at a swimming pool) where dad was posted at the time. Story is that dad was buying a "Baby Ruth" bar at the candy machine and mom was standing by and ask dad for a bite. He gave her a nickel and told her to get her own.

Mom had two brothers; Bill and Burton Bowen, and two sisters; Dorothy Bowen Collins and Mary Lou Bowen Hatton. I was very close to all of them. Some said that I looked like my Uncle Bill and I would take that as a compliment.

Dad was raised in Beloit Kansas and was quite a "hell raiser". I know of a couple of things that he got involved in when he was young and those incidents pretty much told me about his personality. On one incident he got caught after a weekend he locked goats in the school. The goats were in the school over the weekend and when the school opened on Monday, it was such a mess the school had to shut down. He was also caught turning over "outhouses" on Halloween. (Outhouses were toilets before indoor plumbing.) He also got caught coming out the window of a "house of ill-repute" his senior year. That was the incident that embarrassed Grandma Kitty so much that dad was taken to the end of town with a suitcase and pointed in the direction of Fort Riley, Kansas to enlist in the army. That's what they did in those days. Worked out good as dad met mom and our family got started.

Dad played trumpet and was quite good. I also played the trumpet but I'm sure dad was much better. I'm sure he was good because I believe Grandma Baker was very demanding. We'll get into my playing in a later chapter. Dad played in the school band and later in the Army Band at Fort Leavenworth. This picture of him is in the town museum with his trumpet and band uniform on.

I was quite surprised when Darbie and I saw this picture in the museum at Beloit along with some of the old items from Bakers Barber Shop.

After he married mom (Pete, real name Alberta), he played in a dance band around Wichita, Kansas while he attended college at Wichita University (later becoming Wichita State). I think he only went one year due to costs. Mom helped out by waiting tables at a hotel. He told the story that he would play a "gig" on a Friday or Saturday night and after the gig was over, he and the band would go to the hotel where mom worked. Mom was a waitress and during the evening she would save food left on customers plates and send the food up a "dumb waiter" to a vacant room the band was in. That's how they got some of their food.

Dad had one sister (Maxine) who was 5 years older. Maxine adopted two twin girls (Sondra and Cynthia). Sondra lives in Bartlesville, Oklahoma and I used to see Sondra every now and then, but Cynthia lives in Scotland and I haven't seen her since she was a little girl. I do know the story of their adoption but I won't write about it as it's their story to write. I just remember them as the cutest little girls. They were 11 years younger than me, always dressed alike and cuter than a bugs ear. Cynthia became the world traveler and has for the most part lived in Europe and spent some time in South America. Now they're neat ladies and I would love to see Cynthia sometime if we ever make it to Scotland where she is living.

I currently have a rocking chair, a handmade cedar chest, a mantle clock, and several quilt's handmade by Great Grandma Huntsinger in my SaddleBrooke home. These items were brought to Kansas from Ohio in a covered wagon. I also have a lot of Grandma Baker's things, like a piano (bought new with a price tag on back), a secretary, and bedroom set (she always said "this is where your dad was conceived") and other furniture. It would have been nice if someone in the family had this piano for piano lessons for some of the great-grandkids. That would be history repeating itself.

Now For an Introduction of Me:

I was like most of you when I was young. I didn't think my parents knew anything and I wasn't going to let them run things for me. After all, I did all my growing up while making all those growing up decisions by myself and I did pretty well. This wasn't the truth, but this was how I felt. Now this philosophy didn't start from birth. It had to be grown into and I remember that I was in my early teens when I became so smart. Of course we didn't have all the tools at our disposal that children have today. When we got disciplined, we got spanked (me sometimes with a belt) and I learned my lessons pretty quickly. It sounds bad, "spank with a belt" but you don't spank as hard as you can. It just scares the hell out of you. I believe Barbara (my wife and mother of my kids) had a "paddle" that served the same purpose.

There wasn't any police or government telling my folks how to discipline us or even interfere. We also got spanked at school (it was called "getting paddled") and teachers didn't get into trouble for disciplining us. Is it so wrong to discipline kids? I don't think so. In life we learn "what to do" by being told "what not to do". I remembered being "grounded" a lot, but that was just part of the growing up process. The bottom line was that if you didn't do anything wrong, you didn't get into trouble.

As kids growing up, we were able to play anywhere and go everywhere without supervision. The city was my playground. I remember leaving the house on a Saturday or Sunday morning (or anytime during the summer) and when I went outside, mom would tell me that "dinner is at 5:00pm, better be home and don't be late". She didn't ask where I was going or what I was going to do. We didn't need adult supervision and no one was thinking that we would be kidnapped and taken to Mexico and sold. Dad always said, "if someone wants you they can have you." When Donna, Pam and Teri were young, we wanted them to stay in the block where we lived. They did venture out to other blocks when they got older and made friends. Now days, parents want their kids to stay in the yard. Going to the mall with young ones today means the parents have to watch their kids all the time. When I go to the mall today, I don't like what I see. All those teenagers just hanging around practically wearing nothing but a dream. Wow, times sure have changed. In my days, girls didn't even show their bra straps, (did I just write "bra").

I can remember doing things with my friends that would make parents cringe today. We went swimming in the river, rode motorcycles (scooter in my case) all over town and off-road, and hung out everywhere. Yes, when we went swimming we were in the nude. I remember going into a farmer's watermelon field and eating the hearts out of "black diamond" watermelons and getting chased. The cost of going to a movie was nine cents. Don't know why I remember it this way as ten cents looks and sounds better. Guess a penny was worth something back then. My best friend growing up, Shorty, overhauled a car right beside a busy road and I think it took about a week. Parents weren't worried and I guess he wasn't worried about theft.

In my growing up days, school was simply "reading, riting and rithmetic"; we used to call them the three r's. Now you can take a class on how to dress, bowling, horseback riding, sand pile, elephant breeding and underwater basket weaving. Even learned a new one called "Non-Profit" from a granddaughter. Now that's a good one, making a living with a job that's non-profit. Doesn't sound to me it would pay a lot. Don't know why kids have to take all the classes in college, but I think it's really a tool of the college to be able to get more tuition money from the parents or the loan agency.

That's another thing, we couldn't or didn't borrow money to go to college, and I think it's terrible that it's the norm today. It starts a person out in life in debt so much that you have to have a good job to pay it back. It's like starting out after college with an expensive "new car" payment. In some instances it might make more sense to go to a technical school and learn a trade. That way you could start out making a good wage earlier than you would if you waited until you graduated from college. That way, you would be making an income from a company that could help with college tuition. Obviously that depends on which degree you are pursuing. Is there value ending up with a doctor's degree in medicine and start out with a $100,000.00+ debt. What's the sense of getting a higher education if all you are going to do with the extra money you earn is to pay back the government or some agency for the loan?

When I was young, I called my parents "Pete and Parky" and I even called my Baker Grandparents "Kitty and Roy". I didn't start calling them mom and dad or grandma and grandpa until I went to work at Boeing. I don't think this was important to mom and dad as I was never corrected or told any different. As I got older, I personally didn't like calling them by their names and when I was old enough to change, I started calling them mom and dad and grandpa and grandma. I was sure that my kids started out calling us mom and dad. Just sounds better to me. Evidently Grandma and Grandpa Baker weren't bothered either.

Black people were discriminated against and integration was over the horizon. As kids, we didn't know that discrimination existed. It was there but no one made a big deal out of it. Of course, when we were old enough to know about it, we knew that it wasn't right, but our generation didn't just jump into something without thinking it through. We also had to be prodded by guys like "Martin Luther King". The blacks were called "Negro's" or "coloreds". It wasn't a negative classification as the whites are called Caucasians. This was just a category of humans and most people were the same. The blacks have changed they're name several times over the years, so I guess they are still not settled on what they want us to refer to them as. They like or want to be called "African Americans" which doesn't make any sense to me at all. That's a classification where one is from, i.e., Cuban Americans, Italian Americans, etc. Well, most black people today are born in America (just like me), therefore they're Americans just like me. Also Ernie Els was born in South Africa so he is an African American and he's white. I think the black community is confusing originating country with birth.

All I know is that we can't call them what they call themselves. I was never a racist and I grew up integrated in school from 2nd grade on. I didn't know anything else and I remember having black friends as well as white friends. A couple of close black friends I remember were "Ollie Ross" and "Floyd Ware". They even were on my side in a fight one time against some of their black friends. I guess I'm trying to say that if there were racist problems, we didn't know about it and my parents or friends parents didn't think any different. I personally think it's worse today than when I was a child. But political parties keep pushing the button. (Personally I think it's the democrats.)

Growing up, I was more afraid of "Mexicans" than anything else. Got over that pretty quickly when I got into the service. Guess it was because I didn't know much about them growing up. I think race problems today are the result of people like "Jessie Jackson" and "Al Sharpton". Of course those two wouldn't have a job if there wasn't any "racism" in our society so I think they keep stirring the pot. I thought that President Obama could have been a great president because of being black and intelligent, but he was a disappointment to me and I actually think he contributed to our racial relations.

I started playing a trumpet in the 6th grade and took private lessons. My dad had a dance band when he went to college and he had a friend "Cliff Sproul" who also played trumpet. Cliff continued playing around Wichita and had a dance band and gave private lessons. That's where I took my lessons later on.

I always worked from the 6th grade on. As kids we just knew we had to. If I wanted something I had to get it myself. That doesn't mean we were brought up wrong or poor, that's just the way everyone was raised. Everyone worked. Well, most everyone. I don't remember my sister Jo Ann working. Maybe she babysat some youngsters, but I guess I didn't pay attention. Babysitting was what most girls did in those days and the pay was around 50 -.75c per hour. Mom and Dad provided me with the clothes they thought I needed for school and if I wanted anything more, I had to buy it using my money that I earned from working. Not sure kids today think that way.

Anyway, all this just lays the foundation for who I am today and who my generation is in general.

Now for the rest of the story:

Real Early Years —

Darbie and I look back to see how far we can remember into our past. It sure seems like we can't remember much. Is that a sign of growing old? Probably, we have been told that the older we get the less we remember. We've been told this all our lives, therefore we actually started thinking it must be true.

Have you ever tried to remember who taught you (and when did they teach you) to tie your shoe laces, put a belt through the loops, pee in a toilet, button a shirt, how to run, how to walk, how to catch a ball or how to throw a ball? There are a lot of other things in this category, but these highlight the bunch. I mean wouldn't it be great if we could remember learning these things. We just take things like this for granted. Maybe we even think we already knew these things when we were born and just started doing them when we got to the age that we could. Anyway, here is what I remember, no, not everything, but fragments here and there.

The nucleus of my immediate family consists of my dad (Claude Lester - Parky), my mom (Alberta - Pete), myself (Robert Roy - Bob) and my sister (Jo Ann). I was born January 15, 1939 and Jo Ann was born September 29, 1941.

First memory is when I was three years old. I can't really remember if I actually remembered the incident or if I had been told about it so many times that I just think I remember. Anyway, as the story is told, I was on an elevator, heading up to a hospital room the night before surgery to remove my tonsils. In those days the parents were not allowed to be with their children the night before surgery. Can you imagine that today? Today, tonsil operations are just in/out on the same day. Also back then, removing tonsils was considered preventative medicine. Everyone had them out at about the same age. I firmly believe it was best when you see what kids have to go through today. I think Teri still has hers and Pam had her tonsils s out and her adenoids out a couple of times due to some problems. Anyway, I was as scared as any three year old could be and as the elevator was going up, I was going down and calling for my parents. The next morning the nurse asked mom and dad who is "Petey and Parky"? Mom said "we are Petey and Parky". The nurse had never heard parents being called by their names before.

Can you imagine what your child would be going through if they were taken from your arms by a nurse, who would then take that child to another floor so he/she could be put in a hospital bed and wait for surgery the next morning? As parents you would still be downstairs and not allowed to see your child. Wow, that's heavy. Well, that was me on my way to have surgery. The good part of the surgery was that I remember following surgery I could eat all the ice cream I wanted for three days. Just what the doctor ordered.

When I was three I was on the rail of the front porch in Osage City, Kansas, and my sister Jo Ann was learning how to walk and was holding onto the rail as she lumbered around the porch. I stepped on her fingers and she started to cry. Boy did I get into trouble that day.

We moved to Planeview (suburb of Wichita, Kansas) when I was starting the second grade and on the day we moved in, we were all taking furniture and boxes into the house. A group of young neighbor kids were milling around our house and were teasing me when my parents weren't present. Well, a small fight started between some of the boys and me so I ran into the house and told my dad. He took me out to the front porch and as I stood there sticking my tongue out at the kids, (all the while thinking dad was going to get onto those kids), he said "you boys get into a line and Bob will fight each one of you one at a time". That definitely wasn't what I wanted to hear. Needless to say there wasn't any fight and most of us became good friends later on.

As I said earlier, in those days parents weren't afraid to let their kids play anywhere outside they wanted. I remember going outside and mom would say "be home by 5:00 pm" for dinner. She had no idea where I was going or what I was doing. We respected our parents enough that we were home at the time they said. It's terrible what parents have to be afraid of these days. I also don't think that today's kids respect their parents as much as we did. Sorry.

We didn't have babysitters when I was young. I don't know if it's because our parents didn't have the money or they didn't want "someone babysitting" their kids. Probably mostly because folks didn't go somewhere as often as they do today, (patio parties, happy hours, etc.) Anyway, I remember Jo Ann and I being in the back seat of a car while mom and dad were in a tavern. I don't remember how long we were in that car or how many times this happened, but we didn't think anything about it. Obviously no one came along and stole us and sold us to someone in Mexico. We survived.

I remember when I was young and had a dog. Mom and dad evidently had to give it away (I didn't know why) and I distinctly remember having to go under my bed to get the dog for mom and dad. I don't even remember the dog's name. I do remember the prying and coaxing I had to do to get the dog out. It wasn't a special dog by breed, in fact it was a Heinz variety, but it was special because it was my first dog. I remember crying and begging my parents to let me keep it, but they wouldn't. It was probably my first disappointment in a long list of life disappointments.

On the same subject, later on when I was in the 7th or 8th grade, we got a couple of dachshunds named Rip and Rap. While that was what we called them, their real "paper" names" were "Count Von Baker Der Stout" and "Countess Von Baker Der Stout". These were German names as the dog breed originated from Germany. The Baker and Stout were names of who bought them and who sold them. While we'd had other dogs before Rip and Rap, these were my favorite. They were brother and sister and used to go with me on my paper route.

A year later we did get another dachshund (Schottzie) that we used for breeding. That was fun, but we quit the breeding real quick. I don't remember what happened to those dogs, but was told by my parents they gave them away after I left home for Military School. I think all parents tell their kids they "gave" their dogs away.

Rap 

I got the female dog drunk on bourbon one time. She really liked it. It was funny watching her stagger around, especially with their long bellies and short legs. Let me say it was fun to watch them back then. It's dangerous for dogs to have bourbon and they can die from it. I didn't know it back then, hence it was funny. Guess we do a lot of stupid things in our lives and this was one of them for me.

We had several pets when I was young. I remember a couple of black cocker type dogs that ended up with mange. This is a disease that is skin related and the dogs end up with a lot of their hair falling out. Looks bad. Normally today, you take them to the vet and after a lot of money being spent on them (medicines and shots), they end up getting better. Well, my dad just put the dogs out in a "cold bin" we had on the side of our house and they remained in there for a several weeks. He said they would have to get better on their own. Guess what, they got better and lived. I probably wrote about this later in the Pet chapter, so you just might have to put up with it again. Did I tell you I was getting old.

I did steal from a store when I was young. I think most have done something like this. Not proud, but I remember stealing a little metal car and the store manager chased me out of the Planeview Mall. After running all the way home through creek beds and around houses, I got home without anyone catching me. But, mom found out and immediately took me to the store and made me give back the little car to the manager. She wanted me to work at the store for whatever period of time the manager thought was appropriate, but guess I was too young to actually work.

I also stole a leather coat (motorcycle jacket) from a Trend Department store when I was a teenager. The reason I took it was that I wanted my hair to be long enough to wear it in a "duck tail", which became teenage jargon "Duck's Ass" and the coat was part of the "look". Dad didn't like the motorcycle look and he wouldn't let me have my hair long. I would continue to let it grow as long as I could and when I left for school I would immediately comb it into the "DA" when around the corner. Well, I needed a special coat to wear with it to get the "Fonzie" look. (We didn't know about Fonzie yet, but that was the look.) I thought I had a system that worked. It was when I took the jacket that the system didn't work and I had to run out of the store while being chased by the salespersons. Of course there weren't any cameras or buzzers going off to alert the sales staff of what I was doing. But that incident ended my criminal stealing career.

I did not drink a lot of alcohol when growing up but like all teenagers I did some. And I didn't do it very often. I was a little concerned about drinking as both mom and dad were heavy drinkers, and that bothered me. As a result of their drinking, I wouldn't bring kids home to my house much. Not fun seeing your parents drink.

I used to run around with a kid named "Vance Wedell". His mother was a single mom and she would let him drink beer at home. Boy that was a cool mom. They didn't have much money and they lived in a basement apartment. There was just Vance, his mom and his sister. Well, I stayed with him one Saturday night and we drank some beer. Evidently I was still feeling no pain the next morning and went home around 8:00am. As I was coming down the hall to my bedroom, dad called for me to come into their room. All of a sudden I was trying to stand at the foot of their bed without falling and my next memory was I was in their bed and it was 2:00 PM. I got up and made their bed and went to my room to clean up. Took a bath (didn't have showers in those days) and felt better. Came out into the living room and not a word was said. Wow, what an impact that had on me.

Bob & Barbara posing for a cool picture shoot.

Notice cool hat & rolled up sleeves.

We were really cool

I got driver's license when I was 14. Back then, kids worked on farms and had to drive farm implements, like trucks, tractors, etc., and to do that they were allowed to get a driver's license. I wanted one as soon as I was old enough because that's when I got my first "motorcycle". Actually it was a "scooter" called an Italian "Vespa". Still make them today. I remember dad taking me to a "Sears and Roebuck" store (where they were sold) and I bought it with my own money. The salesperson took me to the parking lot and showed me how to drive it. I didn't know how to shift gears or use the throttle. After 20 minutes of training, dad said "let's go". He stayed behind me for a couple of blocks and then drove up to me and said "see ya at home". I basically learned to drive a car the same way.

Dad took me to a parking lot and showed me how to use the clutch, gas pedal and brakes. He only did this once. He then got me a book on rules. I would drive down to the parking lot at a grade school and practice. Then I went to the testing place and took my test and drove for the testers. Passed the first time.

Growing up in Planeview (suburb of Wichita, Kansas) from 2nd grade until the 9th, we had to walk to school every day. No, I'm not going to tell you that we walked 10 miles to school or took a horse or anything like that. But it was probably better than 1 mile to the high school. When we went to grade school, we had to go home for lunch. I was in the 2nd grade and Jo Ann was in kindergarten. Being the oldest, I had to prepare something for lunch. Well, Jo Ann and I got into egg sandwiches. We actually had them every day. I ate them so much that one day while walking back to school after lunch, I got sick and threw up in a trash bin. That got me off eggs for quite a while. But can you imagine it, in the 2nd grade and I was cooking lunch and on a gas stove. Don't think that would happen today. Someone would turn the parents in for child abuse.

We didn't play sports much when I was young. I don't know if it was the fact my dad didn't play sports so he didn't encourage me, or the fact that I was so small and all I could do was run from everyone.

I think one of the better things kids do today is play sports growing up and especially in school. We did play soccer, but it was before school, during lunch periods or after school. We would just divide ourselves up and kick a ball back and forth. It didn't matter if we had 10 kids on each team or 20. We didn't have uniforms, shin guards or special shoes. We just kicked the ball. I tried playing football for a couple of weeks in high school while at Military School. I was tackled by two guys running into me and I lost my breath. Needless to say, at that time, I found out I was a lover, not a football player. I did play basketball, baseball, and track (pole vault) while in St. John's. I was a good basketball player (played guard and was on starting five), but I was just average for the other sports.

There's a lot of controversy about guns today and a lot of people don't want them in their homes. My dad gave me my first gun (Remington 22 caliber rifle) at the age of nine and I was immediately hunting with him and some of his friends. He taught me all about gun safety. I was hunting by myself with my friends at age 11. We were taught about guns early and I'm glad we were. I've hunted all my life and still have a lot of guns.

In addition to my 22 rifle, I have a JC Higgins 12 gauge shotgun my dad won in a sales contest in 1948, 30-30 caliber rifle for deer hunting, 12 gauge single shot shotgun, 22 caliber target pistol, 25 caliber pistol (my mom's pistol), 9mm pistol, 380 pistol with laser, 357 mag pistol, 22 western 9 shot pistol (belonged to Darbie's dad and belongs to her family), and a Taurus "Judge" (a 410 shotgun shot pistol that also shoots 45 caliber). Wow, lot of guns. Yes I have lock boxes and rifles are stored where others can't get them.

I was always a good kid at home with respect for my parents and all elders. I always kept my room tidy with the bed being made every day. The clothes in my drawers were always put in neat and in rows. This was just the norm. Still do it today. Guess it comes from the fact that Jo Ann and I did the wash on Saturday's and when we folded the clothes they were neat and just went into our drawers that way. Do you think parents today would have a kid do the laundry for most of the family at an early grade school age? Don't believe that would happen, too much television for them to watch.

Family was close when I was young. I mean the cousins, uncles, and grandparents. We always enjoyed being together playing or just hanging out. Of course hanging out when I was young was different than hanging out today. We probably got into some of the same kind of troubles, but I don't think we were quite as mean to our elders as kids are today. I've heard some things my grandkids said to their parents I know I wouldn't tolerate if said to me. I don't know why they have to think they should do this. In today's environment, I think kids can get into more trouble than when I was young. Yes we would sneak around and have a drink, but today's drinking seems more serious. Drugs were not a big thing (I knew nothing about drugs) when I went to school, but it sure is today. I think kids today think only of themselves and not others. Maybe that's a location thing, i.e., west coast, middle America, etc.

I came up with this on my own….. In today's world, (and we see it on TV and everywhere around us) there is an element of a lack in parenting compared to when we were growing up. I also believe in today's world, a parent could devote all their time to their children and some of these same children just won't turn out to be loving or respectful.

Saying "Sir"

Guess I've never thought too much about saying "sir and ma'am" to my elders. Being a southern type boy growing up in the Kansas area, we were taught to always say "sir and ma'am" and "please" and "thank you". Being taught from such an early age, makes it easy for us to automatically say "sir and ma'am" as well as being respectful to our elders and most everyone else for that matter. I have seen movies and some reality television shows where the southerners all call most everyone around them "sir" and "ma'am". Without thinking about it, I probably call most of you "sir" and "ma'am". Guess it's just something that sticks with us.

Those of you who have been around Caleb and John-Paul will remember hearing them say both "sir and ma'am" to everyone. Listen closely and you will always hear Darbie saying her "sir's and ma'am" when she addresses others. I think it sounds cute when she addresses me as "sir". When I was young, I can remember my parents constantly correcting us to say "sir and ma'am" to everyone older than us. Of course, everyone was older than us. We sure got corrected when we didn't.

These were the ten (10) commandments that my mom taught me when I grew up:

1. If you can't say something nice about someone, don't say anything at all.
1. Wait your turn to talk.
2. Respect your elders.
3. Don't talk back.
4. Never curse in front of a lady, in fact, just don't curse.
5. Never mistreat an animal
6. Let others go in front of you.
7. Always say please and thank you and yes sir and no sir.
8. Never take more than one (1) piece of candy.
9. Keep your clothes, your mind, and your mouth clean.

I've fallen short on some of those commandants and it usually happens when I get upset at someone. Guess that's normal, but it looks ugly and I usually feel bad later.

Growing up where we did and the times we grew up in meant that when families and friends got together for dinners, children always ate last. It was another southern thing. I can say that I really don't remember eating last, but we did eat at different tables, so as not to interrupt our elders. We were corrected when we acted up and were making too much noise.

Thinking about it today, it's funny I would have been taught to always be polite and say "sir and ma'am" to others and yet I grew up calling my parents "Pete and Parky", and my grandparents "Kitty and Roy". Of course some of this changed when I got old enough to recognize the difference, but the "Sir and Ma'am" has stayed with me for over 80 years. Something about an old dog and new tricks.

Guess that's all I need to say on the subject, except I don't see our youngsters saying it much today. Even though I think it's a sense of politeness I guess I really don't think it's all bad to "not call everyone" sir and ma'am. But it does bug me (being a person who worked in the "retail" world) when clerks and persons who interchange with the public don't call us customers "sir and ma'am". Enough said, besides, I'm getting tired of typing "sir and ma'am".

Playing my Trumpet —

I had a lot of good times playing the trumpet. For the most part, I was first chair "solo" cornet (trumpet) in most of the school bands. I had a rating of #1 in the district that included our marching band on two different occasions. This doesn't mean I was the number one trumpet player in the state, but I was in a group of trumpet players that was considered good enough to be rated as a #1. I wasn't the most technical player around, but I had a real good tone and that meant a lot when playing solos. Early on, I had a trumpet trio and traveled to the different talent shows around town and we competed for prizes (mostly recognition). When I attended St. John's Military School, I was the school bugler and as such I marched with my bugle in both "The Crack Squad" and "The Crack Platoon" during school events. Crack Squad was marching drills with rifles and Crack Platoon was drills without rifles. I also played my trumpet on television several times as the military school would showcase me when we traveled to different towns. I even remember signing autographs. (Hmmm...... wonder if anyone has found those autographs today and wondered who in the heck is Robert Baker?)

My trumpet playing started when I was in sixth grade. Dad had played the trumpet during his high school years and later when he was in the army and when going to College. I don't know much about his accomplishments during his playing days, but one thing he taught me and I believe is true to this day "**A girl hasn't been kissed until they've been kissed by a Trumpet Player**". At least I have always thought this to be true and it continues to work for me. Dad's picture with his trumpet is in the museum at Beloit, Kansas and I didn't even know it until one time when Darbie and I visited.

Dad played trumpet in the Ft. Leavenworth Army Band at Leavenworth, Kansas, and my granddad "Bill Bowen" was a saxophone player in the same band. Guess dad was pretty good because you had to pass an audition and be assigned to play in the band. It was during this time he met mom and ultimately married her and had me. That's a short history lesson.

Dad was in a dance band while attending Wichita University and during that time, he met a man named Cliff Sproul. Both being trumpet players and musicians, they became good friends. Through the years, Cliff made his living around Wichita area with his dance band while also teaching trumpet. Well, dad thought it would be a good idea for me to take lessons from him, so I did. Because I enjoyed the trumpet, I did practice a lot, around 2 hours a day. I actually enjoyed the notoriety and the competition that came with it. And you could do it being small.

When I went to Planeview High School I played in the High School Marching Band. In that High School, the grades were 7 through 12. Not like today where you have middle school or intermediate school. Anyway, in my eighth grade I was first chair. A guy named George McManus was 2nd chair and he was a senior. In those days a first chair from the horn section usually was the band drum major. Since I was only an eighth grader and very small at that, they picked George to be the drum major instead of me. That didn't bother me at all. However, it was this stint as first chair that defined my future in playing the trumpet. I didn't want to be anything but first chair from then on.

Planeview High School - 8th Grade.

I moved from Planeview, (housing suburb of Wichita, Kansas), the summer between eighth and ninth grades to our home on Bellaire Street, and started Curtis Intermediate School in the fall. Naturally we had to compete for who was going to be first chair and I won. It was during this time I had formed a trumpet trio and played in "show trailers" that would go around to the different neighborhoods and have local talents compete. We went from place to place competing until they ask us to quit because we were winning too much. Incidentally, George McManus was one of the members of the trio.

I also played for the Wichita Youth Symphony and became their first chair. Being first chair actually means you always play the melody and any solo's that are required. You were the featured player in the section that you were in. Since I played trumpet, I was the featured player for any trumpet solos. I didn't care much for symphony music as it was mostly for wood instruments, like violins, etc. However I did have some solo's I played and enjoyed. I also played for the Boeing Band in Wichita, Kansas for a couple of years. I didn't get to play first chair in that band as there were a lot of "old" people playing and they got the good chairs. Not fair, as I could play circles around any of them, but it was another of those life lessons.

I then went to East High School for one year (tenth) and I didn't make first chair in that band. We had 26 trumpet players in the band and you just sat down when you arrived at the first of the year and from there you had to "challenge" the person in front of you. Band members would vote on who was best (and just like American Idol, the best doesn't always win). I did make it up most of the way, but didn't get all the way to first chair. I believe I made it to the first section though.

It was when I went to St. Johns Military School that I was no longer in a school band. They didn't have enough musicians to have a band. I became the school bugler and also played my trumpet at school functions. There were several of us students who played instruments, and we would get together sometimes and play. But we never had any formal band. In any event, I have always had fun with my trumpet.

I played my trumpet for a show on TV called "Ted Macks Amateur Hour" which was probably the original contestant show. It featured musical and singing type entertainment. It wasn't the actual show, but a satellite area where clips were provided to Ted Mack to be on his show. I did enjoy doing this. I don't know if the clip ever made the actual network show, but it was fun. This was while I was attending St. John Military School. There was a much younger student who attended St. Johns at the same time who was a singer. He was a young red headed kid, and a good singer, who the school would showcase with me. When we went to different cities, the school would market areas of St. Johns (Crack Squad or Crack Platoon) and also have this kid sing and I would play a trumpet solo. I also believe the contestant Show "Ted Mack Amateur Hour" was a show that had several studios around the country and the one that I went to was Kansas City, Kansas (or Missouri). I played a song called (Carnival of Venice) which is a technical song with 32nd notes, triple tonguing, and double tonguing. Wow, can't believe I remember those things.

I played in the Air Force Drum and Bugle Corps while in basic training at Lackland Air Force Base, San Antonio, Texas. I had to audition and be picked to be able to play. Dad had played in the Army Band and I played in the Drum and Bugle Corps. Similar paths.

While there, another trumpet player (Gary Smith) and I played for a band called "The Starlighters" which was a local band in the San Antonio, Texas area at the time. Gary and I would get a pass to play opposite nights at different military clubs. We got $5.00 a night for our troubles. The Starlighters became a much larger band in popularity that even made records (bet some of you don't remember what a record is) but they weren't that popular at the time when we played for them.

Dad would always ask me if I had practiced today. I practiced 2 hours a day (1 hour each time) every day. I did enjoy playing the trumpet. Guess dad felt that if he bought me my trumpet and was paying for lessons that I should be practicing. What a bummer. I just wanted to play, not practice. Anyway, I think it was the summer between the 8th and 9th grades, and one time too many, he ask me. I got so mad I threw my trumpet against the wall. Bent the trumpet (ruined it). Dad said he was through and if I wanted to resume taking lessons I had to buy my own trumpet. Well, after about six weeks, I missed it and actually bought my own, the one I still have today. It is an English Besson and it has a larger bell which gives it a more mellow sound. It cost around $250.00 back then (1953, or thereabouts). I made a lot of payments on that trumpet. Needless to say, I had a lot of fun playing my trumpet and enjoyed it. The trumpet now hangs in my garage along with my bugle. (The garage is my man cave, nowadays guys get man caves actually in the house.)

In the early years, my trumpet became a financial asset for our family. Donna was born with her left foot caught in Barbara's rib area and as a result, her foot favored left when standing or walking. (looked like a penguin.) She had to have special shoes that were quite expensive for someone in the service, so after I quit playing the trumpet, I started "hocking my trumpet" for money to pay for her shoes. (Hocking meant I took my trumpet to a "Pawn Store" and they gave me money for a specific amount of time and when I picked it up, I paid back the amount I received plus any "interest" that had accrued.) We all know how fast kids grow out of their shoes at an early age and her shoes were expensive (for those times). I believe they cost around $25.00 a pair. So, I would hock my trumpet to have the money. The catch was to pay it off so I could have it to hock the next time she needed shoes. I also hocked my watch from time to time.

Another thing I used to do was sell my blood at a blood bank. I have a special blood type (A negative) and I would get around twenty to twenty-five dollars per session.. You're not supposed to give blood any sooner than every 3 months, however, I used to drive to other counties and so I could give it more frequent. We needed the money. What can I say.

Needless to say I haven't played the trumpet much since. But it was a fun period in my life.

Jobs —

"Love what you do and you'll never work a day in your life"

Don't know who said this, but it's really been true in my life. It's amazing to see what we end up with as a career. People go to school to get their education and while in College they declare a Major. This Major usually sets the stage for "what" they want to be. However, I believe if you look at everyone's degrees today, you will see that the career they ended up with is totally different. Take me for example. I started out taking Anthropology, then changed to Geology and ultimately ended up in Business, leaning towards Business Management. My working career ended up being an "Industrial Engineer" at Boeing, which really has nothing to do with my original scholastic endeavors and I wasn't trained in Engineering. We provided management scheduling and program health. Now I understand a lot of engineers end up engineers, doctors end up as doctors, etc., but the mainstream of people end up doing something different as their careers.

As compared to my generation when we first went to work, I don't think the youth today has work ethics as good as ours. When I compare my youth to those of today, it appears to me that everyone owes them a living. (I know there are exceptions, but for the most part this is what I see.) I never had a job I felt I would be able to keep forever. But If I did a good job, I might be able to stay at the job forever. Lately it seems the consensus is the rich owes the "have nots". At least that's where our politics seem to be headed. Tax the rich and give to the poor. That way the poor won't have to work and will be dependent on the government. I never in my life worked for a poor person and it's the rich people who've provided jobs for the rest of us. There are those who seem to turn everything they touch to gold and there are those of us who work for them. I personally don't see anything wrong with it, but government seems to think they need to keep leveling the playing field. I don't see it that way.

At work, we never took sick leave unless we were almost deathly sick. We always went to work. If you didn't, there might be someone else in your desk when you finally get there. But more than that, we had a feeling of pride about our work. Even when I was a manager at Boeing, I never liked anyone calling in sick when I felt they were not actually sick. I just don't think it's right. That's not what you signed up for when you went to work for your employer. I didn't do it as a manager and I didn't like it when my girls told me they were sick and I didn't think they really were. Ask them…. I always went to work at least an hour before my assigned work shift and usually stayed an hour late. It was a work ethic I followed most of my life. If I have any problem with retirement now, it's the fact I can't sleep in. I always wake up early. Don't know why, as I don't have anything I have to do, but I just can't seem to be able to adjust.

At first, my idea of a full-time job, after I got out of the Air Force, was to wear a white shirt and tie, sit behind a desk and make $100.00 a week. If I could do that for the rest of my life, I would be happy. Not very good goals if you are looking at it today, however when jobs paid $1.70 an hour back then it looked like a good goal. I never had anyone guarantee my job and I was always afraid of losing it. We never felt the Government owed us anything. We did have unemployment, but it was just smidgens to what it is today. I think unemployment was around $29.00 per week (in Kansas). We didn't have food stamps, free cell phones (didn't have cell phones), rent subsidy, programs for women who have babies they can't afford (like WICK). We did have places where one could go for food, clothing, and some basic necessities, but that usually was a church or some local organization that was doing it from donations. Everyone felt we had to work for what we had and we needed to establish goals to succeed. Everyone was in the same boat.

Therefore, I always approached my job by doing the best I could. As I see what's programmed on television these days, I'm not sure today's youth knows what it is to be an adult or mature in this world. I know there's exceptions and those are the youngsters who are not being depicted on television. Kids today might be smart, but that doesn't mean they are mature. (Of course, this doesn't apply to anyone in my family.)

We didn't ask parents for money. Probably because we didn't think they had extra. I do remember one time I really, really needed extra money. Not much, but enough to get me to the next payday. Actually what I wanted was only $10.00, (back then $10.00 was probably like $50+ today). I called my dad long distance "collect" (from a pay phone as I didn't even have a phone in our house) and ask him for the money and he told me "son, if all you need is $10.00, you'll figure out a way of getting it". I think today it's too easy for the youth to rely on their parents. It seems to be the norm. After dad turned me down, I never ask for another dime.

It seems like I always worked. Recently Darbie and I were at my sisters in Wichita and Jo Ann brought up in the conversation that "Bob was always working". I didn't look at it like that. I thought everyone worked. When I was going to school, dad and mom would buy me the necessities and if I wanted anything else, I had to buy them. To do that meant that I had to have a job. Their idea of necessities was one pair of shoes for school and usually one good pair and an old pair for playing. Therefore if I wanted a special pair or something different, I had to buy them. The same concept applied to all my clothes.

I got my first job as a paper boy for the "Wichita Beacon" when I was in grade school. I remember having over 230 customers. On Sunday mornings the delivery truck had to deliver the papers to three different locations because I couldn't carry all the papers at once. Being a paper boy always put money in your pocket. In those days we had to collect from our customers ourselves. We paid for our papers and then we collected from the customers. It was our first attempt at being in business. You had to collect enough to pay for the papers and have enough for ourselves, which is called "a profit". There was always someone who owed money on our paper routes and if we needed some, we could just look to see where we could collect. Both Sara and Lacy had a paper route and I'm sure they learned from it.

When I left the high school I was attending (Planeview High School) at the end of the eighth grade and started going to Curtis Intermediate in the ninth grade, I got the paper route where we moved to Bellaire Street. My address in Planeview was 3930 E. Stearman Drive (now called Durham Drive) and my address on Bellaire Street was 5918 E. Bellaire Street. The Bellaire address was actually in front of the Cessna Airplane Factory. I had that paper route for a couple of years. It was while I had that paper route I met Ken Gehring and later Barbara, my wife and the mother of our kids.

5918 E. Bellaire, Wichita, Kansas – built in 1952

Ken had the "Wichita Eagle" route and he delivered in the morning and evening. We would walk together in the evenings and Sunday mornings. We had a lot of fun on those routes.

**Barbara's home
1919 Lexington,
Wichita, Kansas**

Sometimes I would take my dogs Rip and Rap (wiener dogs) with me on my paper route. One time we were going by a house where a person was getting ready to BBQ a couple of T-Bone steaks. (You know where this is going.) When the guy turned his back, Rip and Rap each stood up as high as they could on their little hind legs and each took a steak off a chair where the steaks were sitting. When the guy saw it he started chasing them, each with a steak in their mouth.

I didn't think those dogs could run as fast as they did that day. It was a site to see. I was glad he wasn't a customer of mine.

After I quit the paper route (thought I was getting too old), dad got me a job at the "Mission Orange" bottling company. Dad was a chemical salesman and he knew the owner of the plant. It was the summer between junior and senior years. Because I was fast with my hands, they put me in charge of the "bottle washer" machine. Guess I didn't do too good as the bottles fell from the rack when going through the washer and broke inside the machine. I was the one that had to go into that machine to clean it out. They used a form of acid for cleaning and it was hell. Even though I had gloves and long sleeved shirts on, it burned me in areas where scrapes happened on my arms and really hurt. Guess that's the price I had to pay since I was probably the one that ruined the line. After that, I hated that job.

Later on that summer, I had a chance to go to a kids church retreat, actually Barbara was going and I wanted to attend with her. I ask for the three day weekend off and the Mission Orange owner said "no". Well, I told dad that I did get the weekend off and I went anyway to the retreat. I didn't even bother taking my lunch with me to work on Monday morning, as I knew what the consequences were going to be. Yep, I was right, got fired. I think this was the only time I got fired in my life.

I then got a job with the school system as a janitor. First worked at Booth elementary close to where I lived and then worked the summers refinishing school desks for the city of Wichita Department Of Education. We would have to sand the tops of the desks to get words and carvings from the tops of the desks, and then spray them with new finishes. It was a fun job, but was real hot in the summer as I remember. We worked in a warehouse type environment which was the reason it became very hot in the afternoon. Nope, we didn't have air conditioning back then. We did make good money though.

I didn't have a job during the school year when I attended St. John's Military School. We couldn't have one during the school year because we went to school five and one half days a week. This meant we went to school on Saturdays for half a day. So, the only times I worked was during the summer, but I did work every summer. I even found the jobs myself.

I remember walking malls and stores asking to see the managers and then filling out applications for work. That's what we did in those days. In today's world, it's the internet. Not only did I work, but my granddad Roy Baker provided some of my early guidance and I remember him telling me that I should always save ten percent of what I made. So, I was saving money all the time from a young age. Good teachings, I think.

When Barbara and I got married, I thought I would just go out and get a job. Wrong. The jobs available were the same ones that I had during the summer months. They usually paid minimum wage which wouldn't support us. That and the fact I figured I needed some more growing up helped me make the decision I needed to join the Air Force. This would give me four (4) more years of growing up, I would make an income and I could start to finish my education. You see, I never thought about anything else other than going to college. It must have been drummed into my head from an early age.

I actually started college while in the Air Force. When I was stationed in Oklahoma City, Oklahoma, I started college at Oklahoma City university. When I transferred to Waco, Texas, I went to Baylor University. I always had to go at night due to my day job in the Air Force, plus I also had part-time jobs. I even took correspondent courses from the government while in the Air Force.

I got out of the service the end of September 1960 and moved back to Wichita. As soon as I moved to Wichita, I immediately enrolled in college at "Friends University" and I was scheduled to start the spring semester in January 1961. Back then, colleges were on a semester system and we had three semesters per year. Obviously I had missed the fall semester. I had a few bucks saved up for my college, I didn't qualify for Veteran's benefits at that time. Dad wasn't going to pay for my education and he told me "I was the one that got married, so it was my responsibility" When I put it on paper, it sounds kind of mean to be that way, but one has to remember that it was the times. My parents were the ones that went through bad times, stock market crash, World War II, and the dust bowl, just to name a few.

I actually had about two thousand dollars saved when I was discharged and I wanted to take a little time off before looking for a job. After I had been back in Wichita for a couple of weeks, mom showed up at my front door and told me to change clothes and get to Boeing for an interview. She had a job for me. I think this was on a Thursday. Guess she was worried that I wouldn't be able to take care of us. Anyway, I put on a suit and went to Boeing Employment Office and got a job delivering mail to supervisor's desks starting the following Monday. On the way home I stopped at a Safeway store and applied for a second job. Got it and started Friday night, two days before starting at Boeing.

I worked second shift at Boeing ($1.70 per hour) so I could go to school during the day and also worked at Safeway ($1.15 per hour) during the day and on Saturday and Sunday. It was quite a schedule. My job at Boeing was the lowest salary that Boeing had and that's what I started with. We drove golf cart type vehicles and Cushman scooters. Not too much thinking went along with this job which was good for me.

One time I was on a mail route that included the electrical wiring shop on the second floor. The wiring shop had rows of wiring boards called "wiring bundles" where wires were strung to become different wiring bundles for the B-52 bomber. The wiring boards were about

30 feet long with aisles in-between. When we drove the golf carts, sometimes we would mess around and cramp the wheel to lift the opposite wheel off the floor. I was in the process of doing this and when the wheel in the air it hit the last set of wiring boards and as a result the boards slowly moved forward and hit the next one. Well, the first one hit the second which hit the third and so on until the last one hit was number 17. (I counted them all.) Workers were running out of the aisles like rats and when the last one fell, it hit a large metal trash container (on wheels) and smashed it. On one side of the room was me and the other side was filled with workers looking at me. Today it's funny, but back then it wasn't.

After a year or so, I got transferred to the teletype group, because of my typing abilities I acquired while in the service. We sent messages to vendors, the government and other Boeing agencies. We were also a "switching center" for the Government, which means that we transmitted messages to other government agencies. We later became a "Crypto center" to transmit classified Government messages. This was fun and afforded me the opportunity to become a "lead" person in the communications center. My supervisor didn't have a Crypto Security Clearance and this allowed me to do some of my studying in the equipment room. That was a big help. I did this until I got transferred to New Orleans, Louisiana on the "Saturn" Missile program. That's the program that put Neil Armstrong on the moon. (Note - When Neil Armstrong went to the moon; the government had everyone's names who worked on the program, put on (microfiche) and delivered to the moon, So, if any of you ever get to the moon, you can look up my name among the thousands on fiche.

In New Orleans, I went to work for Manufacturing Engineering (Mel Lewin became my supervisor) and I became a "planner". In those days a planner worked with the design engineers. We would interpret engineering drawings and translate them for the shop personnel to manufacture by identifying the sequence they would have to follow to build something. This "plan" included identifying the parts required for the build and all the specifications supporting manufacturing the hardware and identifying points where everything had to be inspected and to what specifications. Later I went to work in Quality Control (actually worked for Grandpa Bill Gehring for a couple of days) in a group called "First Article Configuration Inspection" (FACI). During this job I had a job offer to go to work for the government at "NASA", but I turned it down. This was a fun group and I did pretty well at it. It was during this time that Mel Lewin wanted me to move to Seattle and go to work as an industrial engineer in "Logistics Engineering". That was also a fun job. From that point on there is not too much to tell about my jobs.

It makes me happy to see my grandson (Cory Rowe) now working at Boeing and classified as an Industrial Engineer in Manufacturing. I believe he's also called a "Planner" which was where my career started. It will be fun watching him and seeing where his job at Boeing will take him.

It seems odd that I spent more time in this story talking about jobs I had in my youth and my time in the Air Force and not much time talking about my Boeing career which spanned 32 years. I guess since some of you were involved one way or another, i.e., you grew up while I was working there, or even worked for me when I owned mom and pop stores, there's not much to talk about. I was known as a Manager who "took care of the folks who worked for him" and I actually think I helped a lot of people in their careers.

While I'm proud of my Boeing Career as a manager, I'm more proud of the relationships I had with those who worked with me. (I always say "worked with" rather than "worked for" because that's the way I thought. I always thought of my organization as a team rather than those who worked for me, even before it became proper to be a team concept.

I did end up as a "Project Manager" at Boeing when I retired and I was a 5th level manager with a Boeing Base Manager (Tinker AFB, Oklahoma) and up to 350 people reporting to me. I'm proud of my career at Boeing and I had a lot of responsibility. I retired as a manager while most were being busted prior to their retiring. My mom had been a supervisor in Wichita, but was busted during a downturn in the economy, and Bill Gehring was a supervisor for a couple of years, then he was busted. Even Mel Lewin was busted from management and he had been a 4th level engineering manager. So, it was cool to be able to remain a manager until I retired.

There are a lot of small stories I could probably tell, but I'll only dwell on one. Didn't start out good but ended up pretty cool.

I did most of the hiring for my bosses for the organization we worked in. My boss was the manager that originally had brought me into management on the AWACS Program and I seemed to follow him through the ranks. He would get promoted and I would follow. I didn't look to him as a mentor, but we were friends and he seemed to like the work I did and I think he knew his short comings. I think we meshed together.

Well, this particular time I was in need of hiring a person to work in a hardware tracking organization. I attempted to hire a man (who was actually a relative of a person who worked with me). I interviewed him and he had a couple of years in college and was actually a boat designer. He had a dream of building a certain type of a quality canoe or something like that. Anyway, after my interview I went to personnel and told them I wanted to hire him, and the personnel manager said I had to hire a woman as we were not at the numbers we needed to be. (We had to have the right number of minorities to meet government rules.) I started interviewing some young women (who all had degrees and one of them happened to be black) but I couldn't find any of them was better than the man I had interviewed and wanted to hire.

I went back to personnel and told them I still wanted to hire the gentleman I interviewed, and the personnel manager said that I had to hire a "UUF". "What in the world is a UUF", I asked and his reply was that it was an "under-utilized female". He started sending women to me who had degrees but during long their careers at Boeing had always been clerks, etc. for me to interview, and I just about lost it. I decided at that point I needed to call the gentleman I originally wanted to hire and tell him "I couldn't hire him". When he ask me why, I told him the truth, i.e., he didn't wear a skirt. During that conversation it came out that his wife had just graduated college (U of W) and I ask him immediately if she had a job and he replied "no". I told him to get her to Boeing personnel, gave him the name of a person in employment for her to contact and to let me know when that got done.

I then called for her application for an interview. I was going to hire her even if she was 300 lbs., no teeth and couldn't speak English. Well, that wasn't the case, but on paper she was not necessarily a good choice. She was the daughter of a west coast District Manager, grew up with a silver spoon in her mouth and only had one job in her life, and that was a lifeguard. When I went to my personnel rep to tell him I wanted this person, he said they wanted me to hire the black lady, as Boeing got more points for her. I slammed his office door and started ranting and he said "OK, guess you've been through enough". "You can hire the woman you want". She turned out to be an excellent person, made manager in the Program Planning and Control organization where I worked and later went to work in Contracts and became a Vice President. Today she is retired and we've recently visited. Happy as a lark and enjoyed her time at Boeing, just like me. I think she was working at Boeing Everett when retired.

I worked for a man named "Andy Anderson" who had been business manager of the AWACS Program. He was actually my mentor. One time he was visiting Tucson and at dinner, he told Darbie that his only regret of his career at Boeing was "not promoting me higher than I was". I thought that was quite a compliment. I was always a good worker. I was not good at playing politics and I thought good performance would always win out.

At Boeing, I worked on the B-52 Bomber Program, the Saturn Missile Program (Apollo), and followed that by working on the Minuteman Missile Program building Minuteman trainers. I was actually "laid off" from Minuteman (Mel Lewin laid me off) and was hired back on the Minuteman Missile Program in 1972 and from there went to the AWACS Program (Plane with the Frisbee on top) and then to the B-1B Bomber where I retired. I spent 28 years in Seattle, and actually retired from the B-1B Bomber Program in Oklahoma City, Oklahoma. No more jobs.

When I retired from Boeing, I wrote a poem and it was published in the "Boeing News" during the massive "early" retirement offered to a bunch of us employees. This poem identifies my feelings about my Boeing career and I do feel this way.

The following was the way it was published in a Special Retirement Issue of "Boeing News". It started this way: **At Boeing, It's a family affair**

"I've had 32+ years with my Boeing "family" and just couldn't leave (retire) without writing something for those years. It's true, when I think of my years with Boeing, it truly is a family. My mother, father-in-law and mother-in-law, and my aunt and uncle all "retired" from Boeing. I currently have a brother-in-law, a cousin, two of my three daughters and one son-in-law working at the big "B". When I look at my grandkids, I think that just maybe a fourth generation might follow in our footsteps. We're currently located in Commercial (Everett), Computer Services (Bellevue), Support Services (Auburn) and Defense and Space Group (Oklahoma City and Tennessee). I was with Boeing in the good times and left for a while during the bad times. I've moved with the company and have been fortunate enough to travel the globe a few times. All I can say is….there may have been better companies out there to work for, but I've never worked for them. Good luck Boeing."

Robert "Bob" Baker, L-8393
Boeing Oklahoma City...B-1B

It seems like such a short time ago
we went to work at this place called "BOEING"
And most of us back then
didn't even know where our career's were going

Some went to work "just for awhile"
to help us get where we wanted to be
It was either college, going into business,
getting a skill—or raising a family you see

We had our dreams and our goals
RETIREMENT seemed so far away
We felt we had the bull by the horns, and
probably weren't looking ahead for this day

When we look at ourselves today
and wonder where the years have passed
Hardly have had time to take a breath
wow….they really went fast

We've worked on MISSILES
and AIRPLANES with funny looks
We've probably done enough things
to write about in several books

Some of us worked on HELICOPTERS
maybe a BOAT or two
A PLANE with a Frisbee on top
and a SPACE STATION, just to name a few

What makes it so hard about leaving
these friends we've made and have today
Are the paths we've crossed so many times
and chances of not seeing them along the way

We've enjoyed our jobs at BOEING--
and places we've been from time to time
The opportunities we've had, things we've seen
could never have happened on my dime

We've put in a lot of hours
trying to decide what to do and which is best
There still a lot of hours to WORK
but now-- you get all the rest

Now's the time to pass on the helm
to the youngsters left to rise and bloom
and we hope and pray you do a good job
so the company doesn't end in doom

We now have to rely on YUAL
(that's a little "OKIE" talk you see)
At the 1st of the month when I check my mail
there needs to be a check in there for me.

Needless to say I really enjoyed my career and time at Boeing. I always said, "there may be other companies that are better to work for than Boeing, but I haven't worked for them". I really feel this way. I actually enjoyed going to work.

Military —

My Air Force career was a good one, at least for us. Boot Camp was in San Antonio, Texas at Lackland Air Force Base. I remember my first day very well because I actually learned a good lesson. When we got into our first formation, the drill sergeant asks if any recruits had prior military service or military school or any affiliation with the services. I raised my hand and said, "I had military school experience" and he promptly made me "chow runner". That was a bummer because I had to get up 30 minutes before anyone else in the Flight and run to the chow hall and sit and wait for them to call my "flight". I would have to do this while smelling the good stuff that was being prepared. When told to get my flight, I would run back to the barracks and get my flight to fall in and "march" them to the chow hall. I would then call off the troops in numbers of five to go into the hall and I would be the last one to eat. What a bummer. Oh, the lesson I learned was "not to volunteer any information that could bite you in the butt in the future".

Me at Boot Camp – Lackland AFB, Tx (not a Jet)

I am a very patriotic person about the military and our country. In our family, we have my Granddad Bowen who fought in the First World War (WWI), and my dad who spent two different tours of duty in the Army, one during the Second World War (WWII). I also have two uncles, one in the Navy (submarines) and one uncle who was in the Army Air Corps. Uncle Ken and Uncle Rex were also in the Army. My Cousin Danny Hatton was in the Army and was part of a helicopter crew during Vietnam. I don't see anything wrong with being in the service and I think I would have joined up even if I didn't feel I needed more growing up. I still get teary eyed when the Star Spangled Banner is played, taps is played and even saying the pledge of allegiance. Just think of all the men and women who have died for this great country, I think it's something over 1.2 million since the civil war. That's a lot of deaths for my freedom.

During Boot Camp, Barbara lived with her mom and dad. I called every chance I got and I must have called quite a bit as I remember one phone bill (I called collect) was over $100.00. (We did dumb things back then.) Her mom and dad made her pay for it out of her "allotment check". An allotment check is what the wife of a military enlistee would get each month. Hers was $91.00 per month which is an allotment check for a spouse with no kids. So the monthly telephone bill took all of that month's allotment check. I don't remember what my pay was during boot camp, but my back pay when I got to my first assignment was $33.00. I received my pay every two weeks.

Our monthly income was $66.00 a month for me and $91.00 for Barbara which totaled $157.00. That doesn't seem like much today and in those days it was probably poverty at best. After Donna was born (she cost us $25.00 because she was born in a civilian hospital) Barbara's allotment went up to $117.00. Wow, we now could afford a car with payments being around $25.00 per month.

Boot Camp was an enlightened experience for me. I didn't care for the way the drill sergeants treated everyone so when I got a chance, I got out of the first unit I was in. One day, while we were at the "green monster" building getting shots, I heard an announcement made on the speaker system asking for anyone with musical instrument talent to audition for the "Drum and Bugle Corps". I auditioned and was selected to go to that unit. That was my savior during boot camp. As members of the Drum and Bugle Corps, we didn't have to perform kitchen police duties and we got trucked to most of our activities. The other boots didn't care much for us because they thought we had it easy. They were right. We had to play for Airman Graduation every Friday at the parade grounds and practice during the week. But we no longer had to do the things that would help us "save our country". We did have one bivouac that lasted one night instead of the "required" three the other boots had to go through and we were trucked back and forth.

As I said earlier, one of my friends in the Drum and Bugle Corps (Gary Smith) also played trumpet and we both auditioned for a local band named "The Starlighters" and both got the job. They were a no-name band at the time but went on to become something a lot bigger. We alternated our nights playing for them. My parents sent my trumpet as I only had the bugle the Air Force gave me. We made $5.00 a night playing in the different Air Force clubs on base. We had fun. So, in short, my musical training got me through part of my Air Force career.

The only thing I did with my trumpet after that was to "hock" it in Waco, Texas to buy shoes for Donna. You know what "Hock" is. It was hocked for the entire time we lived in Waco, which was about 18 months and I had to argue with the owner when we left to get it back. It cost me $1.00 a month to keep it hocked.

I didn't want any job in the service where I would get my hands dirty. In those days you didn't enlist and know what job you were going to have. You enlisted and then took placement tests. I purposely didn't answer any question concerning jobs where I would get dirty, i.e., mechanic of any kind. I did get selected to go to radar operator's school at Keesler AFB, but I was red-lined at the last minute. So, I ended up going to the 2nd phase of boot camp (an additional 8 weeks) and when my orders came in, I ended up being posted at Bunker Hill Air Force Base, near Peru, Indiana.

After boot camp, I flew home to Wichita for a couple of weeks leave and then Barbara and I headed out for Peru, Indiana. I had a duffel bag with clothes, and she had a couple of suitcases and we got on a train (didn't have a car) and 24 hours later we were in Peru, Indiana. (I still get a kick out of telling people my first daughter was born in Peru.) All the money we had between us was 85 cents in our pockets (didn't tell our parents). We bought candy bars with the 85 cents and I found a newspaper in the train station and looked at rentals.

Peru was a small town and we walked 4 blocks or so to a house on 8th street, which was owned by Mrs. Long. She agreed to rent us an upstairs apartment which had two bedrooms and a bathroom for $8.00 a week including utilities. We had to share the kitchen with Mrs. Long and she had a piece of tape (or string of crochet) down the middle of the refrigerator dividing our food. Our stuff was on the left side and Mrs. Long's on the right. We had to stay in our room (of course we had no TV in those days and we didn't even have a radio) until time to eat and then we would come downstairs. Yes, we fixed our own. Later on we got to know her and we came down when we wanted. Barbara was with her a lot.

I remember Mrs. Long almost died one night. I heard her calling to us from the bottom of the stairs and she was obviously in pain. We didn't have 911 in those days, so I called the police and they sent an ambulance that took her to the hospital. That saved her life but she couldn't come home anymore and had to go to a nursing facility. Her kids were so happy that we saved her life and they allowed Barbara and I to have the entire house for the same $8.00 per week as long as we were going to be there. She was 91 when this happened. As my son-in-law Howard would say, "It was a sweet deal for us".

My first job in the military after boot camp, was being a clerk in the Air Police Squadron at Bunker Hill Air Force Base. (A male clerk in the Air Force was called a "Tit-less Waaf".) A "Waaf" was the initials for "Woman's Auxiliary Air Force" and being a man, I didn't have breasts, hence the name. I worked in the Registration and Identification (R & I) portion of the Air Police Squadron.

The first order of duty after I got on board was to make "fake" Identification cards for Barbara and I depicting our age being 21. In those days you couldn't drink alcohol or buy anything on credit. A car was the main credit purchase in those days as credit cards weren't invented yet. We really didn't go to bars as we didn't have much money but it was a status symbol just to be 21.

We ran around with three other couples and called ourselves the "international" group. The reason for that name was each of the wives came from a different country. Bob Bedingfield's wife was from Ireland, Wasson's wife was from Germany and Smitty's wife was from England. Of course Barbara was from America and that finished up the four couples. We did a lot together and it was good for us because the three guys were career Airmen and that helped me.

Towards the end of each month we would contact each other to see who had food left. One might have hamburger, some form of meat, pasta, potatoes, or eggs, etc. The reason for doing this was to pool our food together so we could have good meals the last week of the month. Occasionally Tillie would send $5.00 and when I received it we would call the others and see what we needed to buy to help feed us.

We didn't think anything about it as everyone was in the same boat in those days. There wasn't such a thing as welfare, food stamps, subsistence for rent, etc. for anyone.

When the base deactivated, I was posted at Tinker AFB, Oklahoma. The reason I got that posting was because when stationed at Bunker Hill AFB, I got to know the personnel sergeant and he was instrumental getting me reassigned to Tinker AFB. That was when I found the value of getting to know the non-commissioned officers (NCO's). The same thing happened when my posting at Tinker AFB was deactivated and I went to Waco, Texas.

When stationed at Tinker AFB, Oklahoma City, I was the "chief clerk" of the squadron. This sounds like quite a big title. The way I got the job was Don Clark and I were both clerks assigned to the 506th Consolidated Aircraft & Maintenance Squadron (CAMS) and there were two clerk jobs. One was in supply and one was in the "orderly room". The orderly room job was for the chief clerk position. The way they determined which one of us got which job was by giving us a typing test. I typed 27 words a minute and Don typed 26. Since I beat him by one word a minute, I got the chief clerk job. We later became real good friends and he named his daughter after Donna. Her name was Donna Sue. (Thinking back, the supply clerks job was the better of the two jobs.)

This posting was probably the one that really started shaping my life. I had a lot of experiences while stationed at Tinker AFB that seemed to set the stage for the "rest of my life". I completed my general education test (GED) up to the equivalent of two years of college, which made me eligible to take the test for Officers Candidate School (OCS). This also allowed me to start college and I actually started attending Oklahoma City University in the evenings. I bought a television set (my first) on credit (17" black and white with rabbit ears) and paid $13.00 per month for it for a year. I bought my first car that was in my name. And, not to be outdone by anyone, we got into financial trouble and I had to send Barbara and Donna home for several months. I did all this while stationed at Tinker AFB, Oklahoma. There were lessons learned and goals set for the future. I made plans and stayed the course for the next 2-3 years until I was discharged.

While stationed at Tinker AFB, I lived at 108 **Boeing Drive.** We actually lived in Midwest City, Oklahoma, which is a suburb of Oklahoma City, Oklahoma. This address is now part of a shopping mall and all the apartments were torn down. You can say I started my career while living in Oklahoma City, Oklahoma and I also finished my career at Oklahoma City, Oklahoma when I retired from Boeing. I found out later that Darbie had lived just 8 blocks from where I lived while stationed at Tinker Air Force Base, Oklahoma. Coincidence….

I got a chance to fly to California (George AFB) with the 506th Consolidated Aircraft Maintenance Squadron (CAMS) and from there I hitch-hiked to Oxnard, California and visited my uncle Bill Bowen for a couple of days. That was fun. I was late getting back to the Air Base where the DC-3 we flew in on was parked, and the pilot made the decision to leave me behind. I arrived at the air strip as the plane was taxiing out to the runway and I started running towards it. The side cargo door was open and the flight sergeant was hollering for me to hurry. I grabbed the side of the cargo door and got my wedding ring caught. Thought it would rip my finger off, but the sergeant grabbed me and helped me get into the plane. Needless to say I had a bloody finger that hurt for a long time. Still have a little scar today.

My squadron (506th CAMS) was deactivated and I got my choice of assignment from my personnel sergeant and ended up posted at Headquarters 12th Air Force in Waco, Texas. Headquarters 12th Air Force was just that, the headquarters for all of the Tactical Air Command Bases in 12th AF. We weren't even stationed on an airbase, but in a brick building. We had to go to James Connally AFB, Texas for any commissary items and medical. I had become a very fast typist (still can type over 60 words a minute) and I think that was the reason I got this cushy assignment. I was assigned to the "Flying Safety" office which came under the orders of the Adjutant General's office (AGO). We investigated accidents and reported on them every month. We investigated all accidents (both major and minor) and even all incidents. What determines type of accident was money required to fix the problem. I got close to the officers I worked for and actually worked close to the Commanding General. One of the officers took a liking to me or felt sorry, I don't know which, and would let me wash and detail his Mercedes for him. He would let me keep it for the day and several times Barbara and I would take drives to the lake or just a drive for enjoyment.

I got an opportunity to ride in an F-100F jet while stationed here. We had an assignment to take a survey of the 12th Air Force work force AFSC's (Air Force Service Codes) and had to fly to each base to accomplish the survey. Major Smith (Flying Safety Officer) was the pilot for this activity and I just rode in the back seat. The entire trip lasted 10 days but as far as I was concerned it could have lasted days longer. It was a ball. My own private jet. You get a different concept of flying if you do it in a fighter and I think those pilots are jocks. To prepare for this I had to go to Luke AFB and take an "oxygen chamber" test and also an "ejection seat" test. That was fun. We then flew to each 12th Air Force base and reviewed manpower.

When the Major took off, he got the plane above the runway and turned the plane upside down and shot up at a sharp angle. I woke up with him saying in my helmet, "Bob, Bob, wake up and look down". When I looked down, all I saw was clouds, and he said "No, look the other way". I looked up and saw the ground. We were upside down. Then I grabbed the "burp bag". That truly was one of my fondest memories from my Air Force Career.

Another good memory while at Tinker AFB, Oklahoma, involved our Christmas the time Barbara and Donna were at her parents in Wichita. I didn't have any money and as a result I didn't have any presents for Barbara and Donna. I was packing and noticed a deck of trick cards my dad had given me and to do some of the tricks you had to read the back of the cards. I noticed some guys playing poker in the barracks and took my cards over and since they're cards were kinda ragged I told them to use these cards. They asked me to play and I said I would after I finished packing. I didn't want to seem anxious. I sat down and played and would push some of my winnings down my pants and later said I had to go. I lost what I had showing and when I counted my winnings, I had $43.00. I bought Donna a trike and Barbara some Baby Doll Pajamas.

I had a chance to go to Nellis AFB, Nevada one time on a boondoggle. The base is located north of Las Vegas, but that wasn't the reason for going there. I didn't have much money to gamble. In those days you could play "Blackjack" making bets as low as $1.00. The boondoggle was that I went to see my mother-in-law's brother "Leonard" and his family. When I first got there, I started gambling at one of the clubs and actually gambled longer than I should have. I had forgotten to call Leonard and when I did I realized I still needed to see them. I ask the flight sergeant if we could delay the returning flight. We both went to the plane and he did something to the engine generators and since he didn't have replacements, he had to order the parts. The replacement generators were coming from another airbase and added a couple of days to our trip. That way we got to stay for a couple more days. Not only did I get to stay longer, but I got to go to Leonard's son's Eagle Scout award ceremony. So many things happen in our lives and so many things we forget.

As I said earlier, I had financial trouble and had to borrow money to pay bills. I had a car payment, motor payment, remaining TV payment and some back rent. Credit was difficult to obtain in those days and the government gave me the money as an advance on my salary, but the trick was I had to pay it back. The government gave me a three month advance and took money out of my pay for six months which meant that I was not taking my full salary. These are some of the big decisions we had to make in our early marriage. So......I had to get a second job. This was the beginning of my working two jobs. I got a job at a HEB Grocery store in Waco, Texas starting out as a "box boy" soon after I transferred there. I worked my Air Force job during the day and HEB in the evenings and started attending night school at Baylor University.

While my job in the Air Force was fun and quite a learning experience, my job at the grocery store was also a learning experience. When I applied for the job at HEB, I remember during the interview the manager ask me If I had experience as a "checker", and my reply was "yes", which was a lie. He had me come in on Friday night and Saturday to learn my way around the store. I was to start work bagging groceries during those two days.

Well, on Saturday the store became real busy and the manager told me to "open up a check stand". I had never checked before and all of a sudden I was going to have to do it on a busy day. First I had to go into the back room and memorize all the weekend specials. Then go to the check-stand and start checking out customers. I ask the box boy "how do I turn the cash register on"? He told me to put the plug into the socket and hit a bar on the register. I then had to get the money tray and put it in the register and start. Well, I did it. Over time I became one of the fastest checkers in the store. HEB stands for Howard Eugene Butt and they are still in business today. I'm sure the grandkids now own the company, i.e., Harry Butt and Ophelia Butt (just kidding).

James later came to me and ask me if I had ever been a stock boy. I again said yes and he immediately gave me two areas ("dairy isle" and "the paper isle". So I went from buying rolls of toilet paper at home to now buying large cases of toilet paper, paper towels, and napkins, etc. I would ask other stock boys what they would do concerning a certain item, and go from there. There's a lot more involved in ordering groceries for a store than ordering groceries for your home. I keep calling them Stock Boys as there weren't any Stock Girls back then.

There were a lot of good memories while stationed at Waco, Texas. Not being on an actual Air Force Base, meant I would be receiving more for separate rations. Instead of the $33.00 normal separate rations per month, I would now be getting $84.00 per month. That was good back then and the extra money helped.

As I said earlier, I worked in an organization called "Flying Safety". We investigated aircraft incidents, minor accidents, and major accidents. I remember these were flying safety categories defined by major parts, money tied to the airplanes or lives injured or killed. We had the job of preparing a monthly report for the General which he had to include in his monthly reporting to the Pentagon. Sounds big. I was a fast typist and that helped me get this position.

We had a Secretary (named Barbara) and between her and I we used to banter back and forth as to who was the fastest typist. So, this ended up in a contest with most of the airmen watching. I typed 91 words per minute and she typed 87. I did this on a manual typewriter and she used an electric which was new to the typing world, at that time. Needless to say I won the money that was put in a jar for the event. Don't remember how much, but I'm sure my Barbara got it.

When Pam was born she came down with an E col i Infection from the milk. At least that's what the doctors said. At three months she weighed less than her birth weight. We had to take her to James Connally Air Base, Waco, Texas, for medical, and after being in the hospital for about a week or so, we brought her home. The next week she was sick again. Took her back to the base and after working on her for a day or so, they wanted to fly Barbara and Pam to Lackland AFB, in San Antonio, Texas and treat her there. I said "no" and called an ambulance and had her taken to the hospital in Waco.

There are a couple of women who played a big role in our lives at that time. One was Mrs. Goldstein who owned half of Goldstein & McGill department store in New York City. The other lady was the wife of a local surgeon who owned a surgical supply company. When these ladies came to the store I always shopped for them. I used to meet Mrs. Goldstein at her limousine and she would give me her list or sometimes walk with me. The other woman always walked with me when I picked her groceries.

Now…..back to Pam. After we took Pam to the local hospital, she was so sick they told Barbara and I she wouldn't make it through the night. I called my parents and they drove through the night to get to Waco. Pam made it that night and we were able to take her home in about a week and a half. Now for the bad/good part. I took her out of the military hospital and admitted her in a civilian hospital and now I had a bill coming. I went to the hospital finance department and ask for the bill and they told me it had already been taken care of.

Those two women had heard our story and paid the hospital bill. I never got to thank Mrs. Goldstein in person as she always went to Europe for five months each year, but we did exchange cards. Of course I thanked the wife of the surgeon.

I had that same job until I was discharged from the Air Force. This is when I went back to Wichita and started the next segment of my life by starting full time college and a working career at Boeing.

Religion —

I'm not going to become a "Bible Thumper" in this book and break down the Christian Religion or the Bible. I'm not an expert and I'm not going to attempt to preach to anyone.

Don't know if you know what "Bible" stands for. It means "Basic Information Before Leaving Earth". And I'm lucky as my brother-in-law is a Pastor and I continue to remind him that he's my ticket into heaven. After all, marrying his sister should elevate me to some status.

I don't think being religious or being a Christian means you have to be different. There are a lot of different religions and each takes on a different light. I also don't think a person has to be constantly in one's face about religion. It's a personal thing with each and every one of us. How you address your belief is your business.

Our older generations grew up more involved with religion than we did and kids today are even less involved than us. Earlier generations and even my generation was more open about their beliefs and most of our history is around religion, some good and some bad. I was and am more involved than my kids are and from what I see of the grand kid generation, today's kids are not as involved as my kids were. I see this as a responsibility of parents. Early on it's easy to push religion by the wayside and concentrate on one's family. After all, we have to eat, or that's what becomes the priority in our minds. That isn't always the case, but percentage wise it's that way demographically, and also in my family. I wish I had been closer to God in those earlier years, just maybe things would have been easier.

My grandparents on both sides seemed to be religious. The Bakers were the mentor I had for my foundation. I still have things Grandma Baker sent us kids and we were always in Church when visiting. I know Grandma Baker's family was very active in their Church community and their world revolved around their church. In the "old days" some church members were "in church" all day. Churches have evolved to what we see mostly today as our Sunday involvement. We used to have services on Sunday night, Wednesday night and Bible classes everywhere in between. We now have Church only on Sunday morning and the Church in our community doesn't even have Senior Sunday School.

With this "pandemic" we are again evolving to a "Virtual" Church with video services on Sunday mornings. I might be able to get into this as I can attend in my pajamas, eat a bowl of cereal, and send my tithe in by using the internet. I can even get up and go to the bathroom without other people in the congregation seeing me. It will not sit well with me if after this Pandemic thing is over, that this virtual Church becomes the "new normal". I hate that term "new normal" because us seniors are not very techi and yet we are forced to accept it. No choice.

I guess I better start by telling the reader **"I believe in Jesus Christ and I believe he's the son of God and he did die for my sins on the cross, was resurrected on the third day and sits on the right hand of God. He will return someday at the end of**

times". And yes, I have read the Bible, from cover to cover. I also have taken Bible classes and studied areas of the Bible. Now, having said all that, I can discuss **my history with religion**. It's probably not much different than a lot of other people of my generation.

I grew up always believing the above statement. Some religions (one of which is the Baptist) really push the "born again Christian" as it states in the Bible and most Baptists can tell you the actual date they were "born again". I don't think I ever had that experience, at least I don't have a date I can put my finger on. I don't remember ever being questioned about it when attending the Methodist Church. But I can honestly tell you that I have always been a believer.

From an early age, I was raised a Methodist. Grandma and Grandpa Baker were Methodists; she was the organist at her Church for over 40 years. (She had her own parking place while the Pastor didn't.) Therefore, Dad was a Methodist and as a result I started out a Methodist. I don't remember mom and dad going to Church much except to watch me play my trumpet, but they always saw to it that Jo Ann and I went. (Dad always said that he went to Church so much as a child he didn't need to go to Church.) They would give my sister and I a dime to put into the collection plate. When we got older, we would walk by ourselves and they continued to give us the dimes. As we got older we probably didn't go as often as we should have. I probably went to church constantly until tenth (10th) grade. That's the time I fell off. (Other priorities.) I remember being one of the workers who helped build the Methodist Church I attended. I would help on weekends by nailing, carrying wood, and in general, just be a flunky. But I did go and was involved to the extent of my ability at that time.

Mt Vernon Methodist Church today. I helped build the original part of the Church where the high roof line is.

My first crack at being in business was when I was attending Church and I came up with a money maker idea. When I arrived at Church I would go to the room where they counted the weekly collection and change for my dime and then go to the drug store and get a coke. I would come back and pick Jo Ann up and walk home. I'll admit I was making money, but I was spending all the profits and my funds didn't last long.

The Pastor caught wind of what I was doing and followed me home one time and knocked on our door. He wanted my parents to know what I was doing. They were surprised, but didn't make a big deal out of it. For a time, they gave us collection money **and an extra nickel** to go the drug store and get a coke. I thought that Pastor was a tattle-tale.

There were years I didn't go to church much and years I went quite a bit. But I have never wavered in my beliefs. At times I was what is called a "Fallen Christian". A Fallen Christian is one that is not being active in their Church at that time. The Mormons have a term they use; "Jack Mormons". As a little girl, Barbara went to the Church of Christ. This was the result of Tillie's mom and dad being Church of Christ members and Tillie and Bill also going to the Church of Christ.

Tillie and Bill went to the El Payco Church of Christ in Wichita, Kansas. I can't be sure of the spelling, but its close. I couldn't find any information on that Church today, so it might have become something else. I remember attending Church with Barbara but I didn't much care for their sermon deliveries or their practice of Christianity. Maybe I didn't give it much of a chance. I thought it was too charismatic. I heard a Pastor say you have to belong to the Church of Christ to go to heaven. I don't believe that way. I'm not trying to be negative about her church, but I just happened to not care for it. I also dated a girl for a period of time who was a member of the "Assembly of God" church which was known to us as the "holy rollers". That one really scared me. There are so many different denominations (I call them flavors) of Christianity, you can find one somewhere you will agree with.

Earlier I talked of going to Military School and part of the daily routine was that we had to go to the school church every morning for about a half hour. It was Episcopalian and we had kneelers in our pews. We also had to go to a church of our choice on Sunday, so every day but Saturday, I went to church.

After Barbara and I got married, I told her I didn't want to go to her Church and she politely told me she didn't want to go to my Church. Guess we were both stubborn. We actually started looking around for other Churches to attend and ultimately started going to a Congregational Church in Wichita and at times to a Presbyterian Church. In Seattle, we started going to a "Community" Church when Barbara got real sick with her cancer. We went there until she passed. The Pastor, Robert Newman, officiated at the services and was with us at the hospital.

I don't know if any of this means anything of who I am, but it suffices to say that religion probably helped mold my life into what it is today. There are people who call themselves religious, some are agnostic and there are some who are atheists and I think there are good people in all three groups. I think all three groups have one thing in common, i.e., "faith". We all have to have faith in what we believe. Because Christians faith is eternal life after this one, the atheist has to have faith in believing there is no life after their physical life (and to me that takes a lot of weird faith). I guess I never quite understood the agnostic other than they believe there is a higher being, but they're just not sure if it's God. But all three have to have faith in what they believe.

Some of these above categories allow us to "not participate". At least you don't have to participate in tithing. Tithing is (according to the Old Testament) giving 10% of your income to the Church. For the most part, in early times, that meant 10% of your crops, etc. Today, it's centered around money. We currently do tithe, but I haven't always done so. There are times that we didn't think we could afford to tithe, but when you get into a pattern, it's easier than one thinks. And I feel much better doing so.

Being Christian, we believe what it says in the Bible and it takes more than just "being good" to get us into heaven. I've heard from different individuals that they feel if they are good and help others, they are "going to heaven". The Bible says to get to heaven, you have to believe in Jesus Christ and that he is the son of God and died for us on the cross. In Christianity this is the minimums that gets you to heaven, but as you start practicing, you find areas where we're supposed to be involved as good Christians. Those come under the category of being good and doing well for your neighbors. You should also let others know of your faith as well as attend Church.

When you get involved in a Church, it becomes your Church Family. As Christians, we should surround ourselves with other Christians and we do pretty well at that. We should also follow the ten (10) Commandments and I feel that I have tried to pattern my life to support those commandments. Like all sinners, I have sinned and I have been a fallen Christian at different times, but never did doubt my Christianity. I don't know if there are different levels of Christianity, and some might think I'm not as good at being a Christian as some people, but I think I am as good a Christian as anybody. Being a Christian doesn't mean you can't have fun and enjoy yourself. I think I have as much fun as anyone. I'll take a drink, tell a joke and have as much sex as anyone. It's all in good fun.

I think we tend to get a little closer to God as we get older. I know some think they will wait until they get closer to the end date to start practicing their religion more. I believe it comes under the heading that when we were younger we were too busy to be involved. As a young man in Lynnwood, I got involved in golf and working on cars. (I had to work on cars to fix what the girls broke.) Both these things occurred on the weekends and if I went to Church, I wouldn't have time to do what I had to. So, Church suffered. Even today, I seem to fit Church into my schedule. I have a rule that I will go to Church but it has to be in the early morning hours and not the 11:00am services. That's because I don't want my whole day to be attending Church. But I still enjoy Church. I think it clears the senses and the Pastor brings me back to earth.

I probably failed as a parent by not requiring my kids to go to Church more. We should have been more involved with Church and set the example. I see that today. Young Life was a good group for teenagers to be involved with and at least one of the girls went for a period of time. The rest was left up to them, and I don't think church became very important during that part of our lives. For many years Barbara had a lot to deal with trying to control her cancer. We all have to place our priorities on the things we cloud our lives with. It becomes a matter of importance. But there was no reason I couldn't have fit Church into our lives more, and I'm sad for not doing so.

Today, Church is also a meeting of friends. We meet fellow Christians for breakfast which allows us to develop compatible friendships. Also, the Bible says that Christians should surround themselves with other Christians and at this time in our lives it becomes a good feeling.

When we first got to SaddleBrooke we attended a Baptist Church for the first 10 years living here. I was gladdened to see the number of youngsters attending Church and Sunday school. When we were young there were a lot of kids in the Sunday School Classes. It seems that as our population grows, fewer are attending Church today than when I was a youngster. I have thought dedicated Christians seem to be fewer and fewer, but I do believe the actual numbers of believers are again increasing. Maybe it's the times. When current events become difficult we seem to gravitate towards the Church. I'm glad I have had Christianity in my life and that I have attended Church for most of it. It has become a part of my life that I expect to always have. Religion, going to Church, reading the Bible, all seems to bring tranquility to my life. It seems to ease my later years.

To sum it up, religion has been a big part of my life and I would like to have been more involved in discussing religion with my kids, but society calls that "interference". Religion has brought me through a lot of bad times and has provided me with a lot of good times.

Pets —

This chapter was fun because it brought back memories of a lot of pets that meant something to my life. Barbara and I and the girls all share having animals in our lives. We didn't have many cats during growing up years, but they are exceptional pets and I've had some I really liked. My grandson Bryan had cats when he grew up and always was close with them. I never had any when I was as young as Bryan but had some in later years that were good pets.

I guess I can't really say I didn't have cats when I was young. I might have been too young to remember. I do remember, what I think was my first cat (was Barbara's and mine after we were married), because we learned a couple of lessons that patterned my life for cats to come. I'll get to this cat on the next page.

I had a couple of little black Cockers when I lived in Planeview (suburb of Wichita). They got mange and dad made them stay in the "coal bin" on the side of our house (had been used for coal storage). We heated with a gas stove in the living room and were not using it for storing coal, so it was a perfect spot for them to use. I don't know how dad medicated them, but in a couple of weeks they started getting better and were able to come out. They basically healed themselves. We didn't have any more dogs until I was a teenager. They were two wiener (dachshund) dogs. These were the only dogs I remember during the time I was at home. I never had pets from that time on until Barbara and I started having pets. I already talked about these wiener dogs (Rip and Rap) in the "Real Early Years" chapter.

I had some unusual pets when I grew up. First one I remember bringing home was a baby raccoon. It made a mess in the house and I had to get rid of it. The next pets I brought home was a couple of baby skunks. I wasn't able to hide them long as they had quite an odor and mom had to bury my clothes in the back yard to get rid of the smell. She couldn't figure out why my clothes smelled like skunk every day for several days and she would bury them and then the next day it happened all over again. It happened a couple of times. She found out that I had baby skunks in the "Coal Bin" on the side of the house and when I would try to feed them and hold them, they squirted. She wasn't too happy.

My next memory was one of catching a snake and chasing mom around the house. I have no idea of what kind of snake it was, but I had a lot of fun because mom was deathly afraid of snakes. The fun only lasted until I quit chasing her and she grabbed me after she told me to take the snake away. I didn't think it was funny then.

Dad was a traveling salesman and one time he went to a sales convention in New Orleans, La. While there he participated in an "Alligator" race. He didn't win the race, but did win the alligator and his or her name was "pink panties". Well, I had the alligator for a couple of years and we fed it dried beef from the store. It got out of its cage one time and mom ended up on her bed and stayed there until I found the gator and put it back in its pen (which wasn't much of a pen). The gator later died; at least I thought it died. It got stiff, so, I put it in the infamous "coal bin". The weather was getting cold and frosty and the alligator hibernated which made it look like it died. We were going to Grandma Baker's for Thanksgiving and Granddad said he wanted the alligator for its hide. We took it Beloit and Granddad threw it out in the garage. As I said, we thought it was dead, but their garage was heated and the gator woke up. He was obviously hungry. He was hissing and making all sorts of noises and running towards us. I don't really think gators were good pets and this one proved it to us. We took that gator to the town zoo in Beloit and it was on display there for over 20 years that I knew of. Used to go and see him sometimes when we visited Grandma and Grandpa Baker. Even took the girls to see him (or her, didn't know).

After Barbara and I got married, we moved to Peru, Indiana (I was in the Air Force and Donna was born there). Peru, Indiana was a lot of firsts for our family, i.e., first residence as a married couple, first kid born, first car purchased, first grown up job, first time making new friends on our own as a couple, first time responsible to only ourselves and first time not being around our childhood friends.

We were going to the store and we were behind a car when a sack was thrown out of their window. I stopped to see what was inside and found a baby black cat. We kept the cat the whole time we were in Peru, Indiana and the cat had the free run of our apartment and the outdoors. That was the first lesson we learned, "Don't allow cats to come and go on themselves". We would leave the window open at night and the cat would come and go. One night he brought home some of his buddies, like he was a member of some kind of "cat club" or something. They were all making noises and obviously getting testy with each other. It must have been mating season. We didn't have a cat box, which is why we left the window open, but we closed that window after that night. It took a long time to get a bunch of purring and screaming males out. Second lesson was the scratching lesson. They ruin furniture. They don't know if the furniture is yours or not. From then on, front claws were in trouble. Don't remember what happened to that cat. I think it quit showing up for food.

While stationed in Waco, Texas, I caught a snake and kept it for Donna to play. I didn't say I made good decisions. Bet she doesn't remember. Had it in a box and Donna would let the snake crawl around her arms and just play with it. Also had a "horned toad" as they are called, and Donna used to play with that also. They aren't actually a "toad" but a lizard with a lot of sharp horns around their head and body. When they get frightened, they stiffen up and puff up their body to look bigger. They also squirt blood out of their eyes when they feel threatened. Donna appeared to actually enjoy both, but I bet today she wouldn't like to have them around.

That snake got away one day while Barbara and Donna were visiting her mom and dad in Wichita. It wasn't in its boxed cage and I lost it in the house. When Barbara got back she found the snake was loose in the house and ended up in my fatigue jacket. She found it when as she was washing it. Man was she mad. I heard her swearing at that snake and me from a block away. She beat that snake with a broom and by the time I got there, it was flat. That was an end to snakes as pets in the Baker household.

While living in Waco, we got a rabbit from someone who raised them for food. It was a black and white rabbit the girls named "Thumper". Wonder where they got that name, maybe the cartoon "Brier Rabbit". We had no cage for it and it had the run of the house and acted similar to a cat. It urinated in a certain spot (under the hot water tank) and I put a cat box there. Problem solved. It also pooped there most of the time. We just vacuumed the pellets that were scattered around the house as they were dried balls, Donna called "raisins". We never knew if it was male or female and but it was a good pet. It would lay on our laps while watching TV and the girls would play with it, even dress it up. We took it to Lake Waco and it went in the water with us. We would put it on a dog chain and it would stay where we had our blankets on the beach. We were making movies of the family by that time and I think the girls have Thumper now on DVD. We did enjoy the rabbit and it was a good pet. I gave it away to someone who worked with me at HEB Grocery store. They probably ate it. Don't know.

We also had a mutt in Waco that was a small shepherd type dog. She was a good dog and we had a doghouse on the side of our duplex where she slept at night. Well, we didn't know what to do in the mating department and one morning when I went outside to let her out of her doghouse, **TWO** came out. We found out a short time later that they enjoyed their night together. She had 11 pups. The timing couldn't have been worse as shortly after the birth, I was discharged and we left for Wichita, Kansas. We got rid of most of those pups and left the remaining with some friend to get rid of the rest. Sure hope he did.

The next pets we got were when we lived in Wichita, Kansas. Got a dog the kids named "Mr. Ed". Don't know why they named him that, but that's who he was. (He was probably named after the sitcom "Mr. Ed the talking horse.) He was a mix as most dogs people owned back then were mixed breeds. He was part Chihuahua, Spitz and Poodle. I, called his breed a "Spoodlecha". He was a good dog. We also got his brother at the same time and gave him to Tillie and Bill. We should never have done that, but we did. They kept their dog until they moved to Florida and had named their dog was named "Bo".

We had a couple of things that happened when we owned Mr. Ed. Saying you "owned" a pet seems callus as I really think they own us. The first incident was one time he got run over by a construction vehicle. We were told by a neighbor who told us they took him to a vet. Guess Mr. Ed didn't know it was bad to fight with a large vehicle. We went to the vet and while there signing papers to have him put down (they wanted $500.00 for surgery). I heard him whimper and that was it. I told them to get that surgery done as quick as they can and was able to pick him up a couple of days later. He had broken his front right leg and it was wired together and he had a cast.

When Boeing transferred me from New Orleans, Louisiana to Seattle, we took Mr. Ed. On the way, we stopped to get fuel in eastern Colorado and Mr. Ed got out of the car. You never knew where he was in the car as he just found a hole somewhere and stayed there. Well, he got out of the car to go potty and for some reason no one was paying attention. We got back into the car and left. About 70 miles down the road, we realized that we had left him back at the gas station. I called the service station and they said he was still there checking out every car that comes in, but he wouldn't let anyone close to him. I had to turn around and travel back. There he was and he got into our car a very happy dog. We traveled 210 miles just to get 70 miles. What a day and not a good time to learn the lesson you have to watch a small dog all the time.

That night we stayed in a Holiday Inn and left Mr. Ed in the room while we went to dinner, (we were not supposed to have pets in the room). Evidently he got scared again and thought he was being left, so he destroyed the drapes in the room. Barbara and I stayed up most of the night repairing the drapes as best we could and we left early the next morning with Holiday Inn not being the wiser. At least they never contacted me for a problem. (I think this resulted from him being left and he developed some anxiety issued over this).

It gets a little blurred for a couple of pets. We gave Mr. Ed away to an adult babysitter due to Pam having allergies to dog hair. (The babysitter gave Mr. Ed back because he destroyed her grandmothers crocheted drapes, so he went to someone else.) Then we didn't have any pets for a while. When we did, we got little dogs that didn't shed.

When we started getting pets again, the first one I remember was a Poodle/cocker mix. Now they call that "breed" a Cockapoo. I was in our Seven-Eleven (7-11) store one morning and a guy came in and in the conversation he said he was on the way down to the pound to get rid of his puppy. I ask what it was and saw him. He was matted, but a cute dog. I told him I would find a home and we did. He stayed with us and became our dog, or we became his humans. His name was "Pepper". Had a long tail, good personality and actually could jump rope when the girls would hold each end. We kept him for long time. He was a good dog. He also took up for the girls and sometimes I would be nervous that he might bite someone when playing. He came down with epilepsy and we went through a lot of pills on him until we got it right. We realized he was going to possibly die sooner than later, so we got a dog from a family friend Cindy Lewin. It was a cute small dog that I ended up giving to a secretary at Boeing.

Most of our dogs were small but I did get a large dog later on. I had a chance to get a malamute and jumped at it. He was a good dog for me. I had never had a large dog as big as "Kobuk". He weighed 135 lbs and could look me straight in the eyes with his paws on my shoulders. But he was a one man dog and didn't much like women or little kids. I tried to make him a good dog, took him to obedience school and had him around kids when he was growing up. I think he thought it was "disobedience" school and he did good. Nothing seemed to work except that I trained him to a command "Front" and when I used that command he would come to my belly button and sit there. Had to use it at least 3 times while I had him to get control. I worked with him every day, but he just had this mean streak. I always thought he was part wolf, but never knew for sure.

When I got him we had a fenced yard. We bought another home and had not fenced it yet so I have to chain him when outside. I had a chain saw party at my new home in Snohomish so I could have some poles and firewood and I had several guys helping me. Some brought their wives with them. Kobuk was chained up to a tree on the side of the house and one of the wives (she knew the dog and knew she shouldn't be doing this) took some water in a glass and part of a sandwich and gave it to Kobuk. She turned to leave and Kobuk grabbed her arm (didn't break any skin) but guess it scared the crap out of her. I made the decision to take Kobuk to the vet the next day and had him put down. I didn't want anyone suing me for my house because my dog bit someone. I cried when I put him down. It was not fun and it wasn't his fault. Obviously I did something wrong. The Dog Whisperer (Cesar Millan} wasn't on TV at that time.

I later got another dog who was the best dog I ever had. Best dogs were always best when I had them so it's easy to say the dog was my best one. It was a cocker spaniel named "Lady". Maybe I thought she was the best because she was the last. I Found her in a TV movie rental store in Cle Elum, Washington. I had seen her a year earlier when she was just 8 weeks old. The owners of the store had purchased Lady first, and then got a sister from the following litter. The sister became a show dog and they didn't want to take time with Lady. Evidently she wouldn't stay home so they decided to give her away. When I went to pick her up, she was matted and chained outside. They said they had to do that because she wouldn't stay home. But she was one of the best dogs I had ever had. She learned to stay home and was good protection for our property.

We also had several couple of cats at the same time. I had a black and white cat named "Felix" and Darbie brought two Pershing cats named Scooter and Sissy Sue into the marriage (who would name a cat "Sissy Sue"?). Scooter ran off and we never found him and assumed he passed on. He was a sick cat (Urinary infection) and cats will often go off and die somewhere. After Lady, Felix, and Sissy Sue passed on we said we would never get another pet. Something tells me that at my age, I would be in the nursing home and the pets would be sleeping on my side of the bed. Not good.

Sissy Sue, Lady and Felix

As a kid growing up, we had to take care of the pets. We had to feed them, bathe them and clean their bed areas. I feel that it gave me a sense of responsibility. It's one thing to ask for a pet and leave the taking care of it to the parents, but when it's your responsibility, you learn from that. We must still be young because we continue to talk about getting another puppy to have in our young "old age".

Cars —

This was another fun chapter because it brought a lot of memories (both good and bad). During the years I had never thought about the many cars I purchased. This chapter represents a lifetime and gives an idea of how many automobiles you might purchase. Of course, salaries are much higher today and the appetite is much larger. You probably won't buy the same ones, but maybe the quantity will be the same or similar. These cars listed are for the most part our main automobiles. There were other cars I will list later that were our 2nd cars. I won't list the cars I purchased for the girls, one of which I actually purchased twice (1969 Buick I purchased for Pam and bought it from Pam to give to Teri). At least that's how I remember it. I told the girls I would purchase their first car and they would purchase the following. Main reason I purchased the first car for the girls was because by doing that, I would pick cars I knew I could work on. Worked for me.

First one – 1949 Oldsmobile 88. Bought this in 1957 when we were living at 108 2nd street, Peru, Indiana where Donna was born. (**Note:** I never had a car growing up that was my own. Instead of having a car, I embarked on my motorcycle career by buying a "Vespa" scooter from Sears and Roebuck. I used my parent's cars when I needed to go somewhere with a date or a group of kids. And we didn't date like they do today, so I didn't need a car and the scooter worked for me.)

The Oldsmobile cost $225.00 in 1957 and I couldn't purchase it on credit because I had not established credit at that time. The bank didn't want to take a chance on me as I was young. We didn't have credit cards in those days and the only place you could get credit was either at the Bank or in-store credit. I did make fake ID's saying Barbara and I were 21, but that didn't seem to help. In those days we could have credit if we were over 21 as we didn't have VISA at that time. Since credit was either a bank or store credit only, getting credit was not a given. (Probably should be that same way today.) Most of what we purchased we paid cash for. (Remember cash?) Because of not being able to get credit on my own, I had to have a person co-sign for me. He was my NCO Staff Sergeant named Albert Hirn. He later ended up in a mental institution and I had to go through a lot of paperwork to get the title in my name. I sold that car in Oklahoma City and the person who bought it promptly totaled it in a wreck two blocks from where he took ownership. Must have been a black cloud over his head or something like that.

2nd Car – 1953 Oldsmobile Holiday 88 – Bought this car from a Major in the service. Cost $450.00. This was a neat car and a good one for us on a low income. I kept this car until I got out of the service for many years and even had to put in a new engine, which cost us $250.00. I would sneak onto the flight line at night and put Jet Engine fuel into the gas tank. Of course it was not leaded and ultimately it ruined the engine. P.S., as I was using a five (5) fingered discount and the fuel cost me nothing.

3rd Car – 1959 Ford – This was a car I purchased from a person who worked at a "Service Station" or "Gas Station" (called that because they would actually perform service on your car when you purchased gas, i.e., wash windows, check oil and tire pressure and even say thank you). The guy who owned the car before me was the son of a Police Chief of a small town who only kept his patrol car for 1 year and then sold it to his son who owned it for a couple of years. So, he sold it to me. I believe I paid around $1,000.00 for it. It had, a 421 cubic inch engine, with an oversized automatic transmission and a 411 rear end. All that made it fast. I'll have a story about that car in a future chapter that involved my dad.

4th Car – 1963 Chevy II Nova station wagon – This was the first **"New"** car I purchased. Bought it when we lived in Wichita and while I was attending college and working at both Boeing and Safeway. It was red and we "ordered" the car. We paid around $2300.00 for it and it became the last car we purchased without air-conditioning as it was fairly new and only an option at that time. We had this car when we moved to New Orleans in 1963. In those days, when you purchased a new car, you kept a pad and pencil by your side and for the first six weeks you would write everything down that needed fixing. You then took the car back to the dealer to get those things fixed. Times have changed. Today's automobiles are much better. I've purchased many cars that I never had to have any warranty work done while I owned them. Times have changed.

5th Car – 1965 Chevy Impala – Purchased for $2900.00. In those days I used Dad's philosophy about car buying. He was a traveling salesman and said that since cars are guaranteed for 2 years or 24,000 miles you might as well get one every two years. That way you won't have much service to deal with and it will be under warranty the whole time you have it. While I didn't keep this car a real long time (4 years), it was the first car I kept until it had over 100,000 miles on it. That's a lot of miles, but I bought it in Wichita when living in New Orleans and shortly after I got it I was transferred to Seattle, Washington and I took a vacation right after I located there. The vacation was to California, stayed with my Uncle Bill and went to Disneyland and sightseeing. Put a lot of miles on it the first year we had it.

6th Car – 1968 Buick Skylark Station Wagon – This is the third new car I purchased and the first car I kept a long time. We actually had it for about 7 years. Had a hitch installed so I could pull a travel trailer. That car went a lot of miles and saw a lot of territory and we spent many a good vacation in that vehicle. In fact I have a couple of stories.

We started on a six week vacation with just me and the girls for the first couple of weeks, as Barbara only had a month off. I often think of that time today. Barbara flew into Wichita, Kansas and met us and we continued on our trip. My "one on one" time with the girls was and is to this date one of the most precious times I had. Of course they probably only remember the times I might have become upset with them, but I remember a whole lot more.

I don't remember how much that car cost, but the monthly payments were $98.00 (which was the most I had paid for any car payments). I never understood why anyone would have car payments that high. I only made payments for about a year. At the time, I owned a 7-11 which taught me how to purchase and pay cash. After that I never had another car payment. If I couldn't pay cash for it, I didn't buy it.

7th car – 1973 Oldsmobile 88 – This was the first **used car** I purchased (after buying new ones) as my main car and I was nervous. I had them write something in the contract identifying I had six weeks to check out the ride and they would have to fix everything I found wrong. That bit them in the behind as they had to tune it up, fix the carburetor, and fix the radio. This turned out to be a real good car and one I really enjoyed. Also had it outfitted to pull a travel trailer. We kept this car for about 7 years. Nothing spectacular but was a good car. I believe we only paid $1800.00 plus a trade in..

8th Car – 1979 Chrysler Cordoba – First Rental Car I purchased. We purchased it from Hertz. Was a good car and would have kept it for a long time, but got hung up on buying the next one. Don't remember too much about this car except the front end was long and I thought it looked great.

9th Car – 1981 Dodge "Trick" Van – Bought this van new. This was my attempt at having a vehicle I could travel and sleep in. It was really outfitted. It had a built in closet, refrigerator, sofa that made into a bed, 4 captain chairs with a table for eating. Only kept this vehicle for about 18 months, but did my share of traveling. We even pulled a travel trailer with it.

10th Car – 1983 Lincoln Town Car – First Lincoln I owned. Originally belonged to the wife of the Ford Dealer in Everett, Washington. It was only six months old when I purchased it and I had it a long time. Had over 118,000 miles on it when I traded it for a Nissan Maxima in 1992. It was a real comfortable car and I liked traveling in it.

Darbie had a hard time driving this car because it was too big. She never was able to parallel park that car. Later she told me she was never able to parallel park any car. One day when she went to work, I called her office and her boss answered the phone. I asked to speak to Darbie and he said "here she comes..., she's looking..., no..., there she goes..., but she'll be back". She was actually looking to see if she could park in a forward parking spot in front of the office. Her boss said she had been traveling around the complex several times. When she called me back later she said it took quite a long time for her to get into the office. She then started riding with our next door neighbor who also worked for the Navy and that took care of the problem. Of course I always say that Darbie never "drives" a car, she only "aims" a car.

11th Car – 1992 Nissan Maxima – This was a real fun car. Had my first "sun roof" and had it outfitted with special leather seats and leather side panels. It was fast and fun to drive. Donna liked the spoiler on the back. It was soft and she liked to squeeze it.

12th Car – 1993 Toyota Tercel – This was actually purchased as a 2nd car, but became my only car when we purchased the Motor Home in 1994. It was also a rental car purchased from Hertz. We paid

$10,000.00 for it. I had traded in our Maxima for the motor home and this resulted in us having only one car which we pulled behind the motor home. This is the first car we gave to the grandkids. We gave it to Donna and Howie for Sara to drive as she was the oldest grand kid. I don't think the car was a money saver for Donna and Howie.

13th Car – 1995 Toyota Camry – Bought this car because we were getting ready to retire. We were living in Edmonds, Oklahoma and we purchased it through Costco. You could go to Costco and see what dealers sold under the Costco name. In those days the dealer let you purchase the car for 5% over invoice. That was good in those days. We had that car for over 70,000 miles. One of the best new cars I ever purchased. We didn't have to spend a dime on that vehicle other than oil changes. It cost us around $18,500.00.

14th car – 2000 Dodge Durango – Darbie's brothers childhood friend "Jim Click" owns 11 dealerships in the Tucson area and more in California. Called him and told him what we wanted and he actually got the car for us and we bought it for a lot less than a dealer would sell to someone else. He still made money or he wouldn't have sold it to us. Ken made a trailer hitch plate cover for that car. That trailer hitch now resides on our "golf cart". This car cost us $32,000.00. We took a trip to Seattle for Thanksgiving and decided to just show up for the meal at Pam's house and surprise the kids. We parked the car across the street in a driveway (cult a-sac) and parked it in head first. We were hiding in the garage and I heard Ken say, where is Bob and Darbie? Forgot the Arizona tags on the car and he saw them. (Note: Notice that these cars are getting more expensive.)

15th Car – 2001 Lincoln Town Car – Also bought this car from Jim Click. It cost us $32,000.00. We had gone to Las Vegas with another couple in their Cadillac and it was real nice riding. After we got back, Darbie said maybe we should get a luxury car. I told her to call Jim Click (one of his dealerships is Ford/Lincoln) and she told him she wanted a new car. He asks what kind and she told him "the biggest one they make". He wanted to know what she wanted on it, and she told him she wanted it "like a hamburger – with everything". It took him two months to find the car she wanted and one day in January 2001, he called and said our car was in. I was nervous. It was a Lincoln Town Car (Cartier) and was a really good car. We kept it until we had over 108,000 miles on it when we replaced it. It was starting to become costly to keep. Don't get me wrong, it was one of the best cars I had owned, but it was time to replace it.

16th Car – 2010 Lincoln MKS – Cost us $39,000.00, and have times changed. Bought from (you guessed it), Jim Click. We had made up our minds that we would buy a 2010 MKZ. It's was a little smaller car and when Darbie got inside a MKS, she said "this is the one I want". So, you know how that goes, we got the MKS. Loved it. First car we owned that was heading into the high-tech world.

17th Car – 2015 Lincoln MKX – Cost us around 38,000.00. **Thought it would probably be my last automobile.** Darbie said when she quit working she thought we needed to get an SUV. So we got an SUV. Sure drove nice. Again, bought it from Jim Click. He sure has saved me some money over the years, plus being a good friend. The main thing I get from Jim Click is that I work with the Manager of the dealership instead of a salesman and I get all the discounts available to Jim (kick-backs, etc.) and I don't have to haggle. (P.S. Darbie still hasn't quit working.)

18th Car – 2019 Lincoln Nautilus – **Nope the last one wasn't the last one.** We purchased this and as of now it's the best one. Just like pets, the last one is always the best. However now, they're more high tech which becomes a problem for us seniors. Having a car smarter than me is embarrassing sometimes. Paid $39,000.00 for it. We probably would have a lot more miles on it, but due to this Pandemic thing, it hasn't been on the road as much. The jury is still out, but it has a lot of features that all senior's should have in a car.

It almost drives itself, lets me know when it drifts and has radar to make sure I keep back a certain distance. It also stops by itself which is a good reminder for me. Only problem, we're not as "techi" as you youngsters. Remember, the only thing techi we had to grow up with was "Party Line telephones". We only had to know how many rings our party line was and only answer it on our rings. (Ours was 2 rings)

This represents all the "main" cars we purchased in my lifetime. Haven't figured up the cost, but I'm sure it's a lot of money when added up. Can't believe I only bought 18 main cars. That means I purchased a new (some used) car every 3.5 years (every 42 months). Like I said earlier, dad always told me to buy a new car every 2 years.

Our first home cost 12,500.00 and our last car cost $39,000. Something wrong with that story.

Got to be a couple I missed….. Have to think on it.
The following cars were purchased as 2nd automobiles.

1949 Plymouth – My hunting vehicle

1955 Pontiac –

1963 Toyota Corona – (I called it a Toyota Coronary). We had this car for 9 years and it was probably the best automobile purchase I ever made. We Bought it for $961.00 from Ray Purington (Frankie's third husband) and it went through all 3 girls who each wrecked or did some damage. (I know someone will come to me and say "I didn't". Had it for nine years. We sold it for $650.00. Best car value I had.

1961 Chevy – I painted this car in my garage and used the motor for a 1964 Chevy I purchased for Donna. The 1964 Chevy was stolen from my driveway and used in a robbery of a 7-11 store and wrecked during that robbery.

1958 Dodge Convertible – not good in Washington

1973 Ford Pickup – Gave to son-in-law Mike Ross (think it cost him money).

1975 Ford Pickup -

1979 Ford Pickup – Gave to son-in-law Ken Rowe (probably cost him money).

1997 Suzuki Jeep -

1993 Toyota Tercel – became our main car for a while and gave it to Sara. Probably a pain in the butt for son-in-law Howie Hughes.

1995 Mitsubishi Pickup -

1995 Nissan Altima -

1993 Pontiac Grand Am – Purchased from Grandma Tillie and gave to Amanda when she was attending college.

(Probably the best automobile I gave to my family).

2001 Ford Mustang (red) Convertible – Bought when we sold our motorcycle.

2007 Ford Mustang (black) Convertible -

2012 Mercedes Benz E-350 Convertible - Purchased in a senior moment.

I imagine the sons-in-law have stories to tell about the vehicles I gave them, but they can write about it in their stories and I hope they wait until after I'm gone.

I purchased 16 second (one every 3.9 years) vehicles, some used by everyone (like the 67 Toyota which was used by all three girls) and some I drove to work. That's a total of thirty five vehicles (one purchased every 2.8 years).

Mel Lewin was my mentor on working on automobiles and was usually around when I did. I was not a good mechanic but I wasn't afraid to at least attempt to work on them. I changed engines, overhauled engines, did normal maintenance, fixed brakes, etc. It became a stress relief for me. I had an engine puller in my garage and also painted 3 vehicles in that garage. It was my second home. Needless to say, my garages were working garages not showplaces.

Note: I feel I need to say my father-in-law (Bill Gehring) was always with me when I tackled anything. He became my life long best friend and we did everything together. He started me playing golf, we took vacations together, he usually went hunting with me and we became a partner in the 7-11 stores together. After our retirements, he and Tillie moved to Tucson to be near us and unfortunately he died 6 months after they moved into their new home. He was the one family member that wasn't critical of me when I went through my bad times. He may not have supported me during my bad time but he didn't feel it was his place to criticize. I truly loved this man........

School – Some good and some bad

Most of this is good. The part that's bad I'm not proud of but it was part of my life and believe me, I learned from it. We will all have times in our lives we're not proud of. It's all in how you grow from it.

Guess I almost flunked kindergarten. Mom used to tell the story that the kindergarten teacher came to see her one day and told her I was going to be held back. Mom wasn't going to let me flunk kindergarten and told my teacher that if I flunked anything, it was going to be a grade not kindergarten. She talked the teacher into not flunking me and evidently I straightened up as I never flunked a grade. Got close but didn't. I think I was pretty smart in school. I didn't have to work hard to get decent grades. Hope some of that got passed on. I think Donna, Pam and Teri were pretty smart, but this isn't about them. I remember my sister making straight A's. She was pretty smart. I always just wanted to make passing grades. I didn't want to waste my time trying to make straight A's.

I don't remember kindergarten and 1st grade. I went to Will Roger's elementary school in Planeview starting in the 2nd grade. Dad had taken a job with "The Diversey Corporation", (a chemical company), as a salesman and that took us to Wichita. Our schools were already integrated back then so I can't tell you much about integration. There was still integration in the south and the first time I got exposed to it was when I was in boot camp stationed at San Antonio, Texas. That will be discussed later.

I had black friends, (in those days they were called "colored"), and the ethnic group we didn't know much about was the Mexicans (or Spanish). We didn't call them colored even though today they are referred to as "persons of color". Persons of color weren't called "African American" or "Hispanic American" back then. Since they were all born in the United States, they were American's just like me. I don't know what they gain by wanting to be identified as anything but "Americans". I still to this day do not like calling people by their ethnic groupings unless they were actually born where they're referenced as being from. I have more German in me than President Barrack Obama has black in him, but I don't refer to myself as a "German American".

I don't remember anything about Asians being in our schools, (even through high school), when I grew up nor did we live around any. All of us kids did get into fights, (we probably had a tendency to stick within our own groups), with each other, but I don't remember being racial about it. One time I got into a fight with some black kids and couple of my black friends helped me.

We didn't have sports during my early years like they do now. We played soccer but it was a game to play during recess or before/after school. The first school sports I played was when I attended Military School in the 11th grade. I was a pretty good student and actually was a pretty good kid. I played football (for 2 weeks), baseball (outfielder because I could hit pretty good), track (pole vault because I didn't like to run) and basketball (my best sport). My football career was cut short because I was an end and the first time I went up to catch a ball I got sandwiched by two tacklers and had to be carried off the field. That was it. I decided I was going to be a lover, not a football player. In baseball, I didn't have reflexes fast enough for infield. But

I could hit the ball and they wanted me on the team, so I was put in outfield. I did better in this sport. I wasn't good in track. In basketball I was on the starting five playing guard. This was my best sport. In those days we couldn't travel or palm the ball like they do today. I wasn't much of a scorer but I was a good ball handler and had a lot of assists. I did win one game throwing the ball from center court in the last seconds of a game and did make the basket winning the game. That was fun.

Since we were always integrated, I didn't especially think things were different. We actually called blacks "coloreds" in those days. They also called themselves colored. We used to get into fights, blacks against whites and Mexicans against whites or blacks, but that was as close to gangs as we had. Coloreds lived in the North West part of Planeview and I think the Hispanics lived anywhere they wanted. One of my best friends in my neighborhood was a Mexican family named "Ortega" They liked me and I really liked them. They would feed me Mexican food at times when I lived in Planeview. This was my first exposure to Mexican food.

I started high school in the seventh grade at Planeview high school. Planeview High were grades seven through twelve. I only went there from seventh and eighth grades. Moved to Bellaire Street and started Curtis Intermediate in the ninth grade. It was there I first met Barbara. Actually went steady with her for two weeks in the 9th grade until she broke up with me. She was my high school sweetheart. Unusual to marry someone you went with during high school, however, Sara and Ryan were high school sweethearts also. We have that in common.

I started the tenth grade at East High School. Played trumpet in the band and actually moved from last section the first section by constantly challenging the guy in front of me. We had challenging every Monday morning and I usually challenged the guy in front of me most weeks. From here I'm not too proud, but it was a time in my life that I had to deal with.

I actually got kicked out of high school at the beginning of the eleventh (11th) grade. I was in an English class and the teacher and I got into a heated discussion that resulted in her throwing her car keys at me. I think I threw an eraser at her (or something like that) and stormed out of class. Now, this school was a big school. It probably had something like 4,000 students. Well, when I walked out of class, I ended up walking into the Principal "Mr. Moore". Wonder what the odds of that were. I was out of school for a couple of weeks and my mom and dad was furious with me. Not only did I get kicked out of the High School, but I was suspended from going to school anywhere in Wichita school district. That was serious. What followed changed my life as far as education was concerned. Here I was, a sixteen-year-old boy that probably looked like I had no future at all.

After I got kicked out of school, dad had told me that I had one of two choices, (1) to go to Military School and since I had screwed up, he would take money out of my savings account to help pay, and (2), go into the military. I wasn't smart enough to know that I couldn't go into the military at 16. He said he could sign the papers allowing me to go.

About this same time, dad had an accident in his company car and it was in the body/repair shop in Augusta Kansas, which was close to Wichita. It was being repaired at the Chevy dealership. Dad asked me to go with him to pick up his car. That way, I could drive one of the cars back. When we got there, he started talking to a guy washing cars. The guy had just been discharged from the Navy and dad started asking him questions about his life. He said he was working for seventy-five cents an hour washing cars because that's all he could do. He had quit school and gone into the military and now was sorry that he did this. Now I'm sure dad had this set up, but I wasn't smart enough to figure it out. All I heard was that this guy had problems getting a job because he hadn't finished school.

I drove the family car home and when dad got there a while later, I told dad I wanted to go to military school. Dad ended up taking $1100.00 out of my savings account to pay for the tuition which was $2500.00 a year at the time. The school was St. John's Military School at Salina, Kansas. It was a good school and unfortunately closed its doors in 2018 and tuition was $25,000.00 a year the last year. I got a scholarship to go my second year. I think military school changed my thinking and framed my life from that point on.

Military school was fun as well as providing a good education. We started school two weeks earlier than public schools, and had a spring break (back then public schools didn't have one) and actually got out of school a couple weeks earlier. Guess that's because we went to school a half day on Saturday's. The school actually closed in 2019.

Jo Ann and I in Beloit, Ks with my St. Johns Military School uniform, Salina, Kansas.

Good Looking in my uniform.

When in public school I had been taking courses like Elephant Breeding, Sand pile, and Basket Weaving and after starting a month late at St. Johns, I was taking courses like Latin, Calculus, sciences, etc. And while those classes were harder, I even got a partial scholarship to go the following year. I really enjoyed going to a private school. We had our own dorm rooms, wore uniforms (we were affiliated with the Air Force), and we felt we were on our own while at school. With Military School came a whole new set of trouble we could get into.

The first night at St. Johns, I was dropped off around 8:00pm and shown to my dorm room. I was introduced to my roommate and told which bunk was mine and which desk was mine and which closet was mine. Then the officers left the room. I didn't want the assigned bunk, closet or desk. I was just being a jerk and that didn't go over very well with my roommate and we got into a fight. Now, I could handle my own as long as it was a street fight and I could bite and scramble. Officers came into our room and broke up the fight and promptly took us over to the gym. There, they put gloves on our fists and rang the bell and we started fighting three minute rounds. If you haven't fought in three minute rounds, you're missing something. It really tires you out fast. Anyway, I got my bottom teeth chipped and he knocked me out in the third round. At least I think I was knocked out.

We dated local girls from Salina, Kansas. I think the parents like their daughters dating us because they might have thought we were rich kids. We only got a weekly allowance of $2.00 so we didn't have much to spend. These parents would let us drive their cars and would even pay for some of the dates. Good set up.

However, that didn't set well with the local boys in public school in Salina, so we constantly had confrontations we had to deal with. When you walked around town, going to the theater, stores, etc., the local boys would yell at us and occasionally we would have a scuffle or two.

We had a student in our school from Rapid City, South Dakota who had worked in a reptile zoo. He actually purchased a Boa Constrictor from somewhere and when it came to the school, it was crated in a figure eight. He purchased a cage, but we had to get that snake out of the crate, remove ticks and get him (or her) into that cage. Next we had to feed it. Rather than purchase food it all the time, we would sneak out at night and go down to a Bani Chicken farm a couple of blocks away and steal a couple of chickens. Then we put them in the cage with the snake and they would remain there until sometime we looked at that snake and he had a couple of bulges.

Think I said earlier that I was the school bugler and played in the Crack Squad and Crack Platoon. As bugler, I got all students up in the morning, played at all formations, called students to education, mess hall, and put them to bed at night.

The end of the year retreat formations were usually done with some creativity. One time I ask another trumpet player on the other side of the school and as I played Taps, the other trumpet player to echo my notes from the other side of the building. Sounded pretty good and gave a person goose bumps.

When the school year is getting towards the end of the year, the teaching staff would take seniors out for a meal and some congratulations. I thought since there were no faculty, nor any seniors around, I would use that time to have some fun. So.... I played "To The Colors" on my bugle with a little "blues" in the music. Bad choice. The faculty and seniors hadn't left yet and heard what was going on and guess what.......Yep...Baker got into trouble.

We did travel as a school and put on crack platoon drills and crack squad drills at schools and on TV. When we did those things we were actually marketing the school. Like I said earlier, I would usually play something on my trumpet like a solo or something with a piano accompanist. There was a young red haired kid in lower grades who was a real good singer. Both of us would be put on TV for different segments. It was fun and I actually signed a few autographs.

When I got to St John's I was still one of those smart ass teenagers who didn't like authority. At military school, they treat it differently.

When you break the rules you get "gigs" which resulted in 15 minute walks around the flag pole in front of the school and you did this when 1 hour of combined time was met. You could also elect to perform some duty for an officer, or teacher as outside work. These are things like cleaning up an officer's room, polishing his shoes, etc. Well, I had 77 gigs against me before Thanksgiving and was almost set up to be kicked out of school. Dad and mom came up at Thanksgiving and couldn't take me off campus grounds to go out to eat. I straightened up pretty fast after dad talked to me.

I think I told you I had to pay for as much of the tuition as I could out of my savings. Tuition was $2500.00 per year and I had something over a $1,200.00, so dad took $1100.00 to help pay. On top of tuition we also had to pay for uniforms and some outside activities. Dad must have paid for that.

Dad had to pay $84.00 for a pair of shoes for me that were required for school. He wasn't much excited about that and promptly went out and bought a pair for himself. He said they were the most uncomfortable shoes he had ever worn. Eighty four dollars was a lot of money in those days.

Dad was a traveling salesman and knew a lot of people. When working and staying In Salina he would stay at the Wymore Motel. That in itself doesn't and won't mean much to you, however, Pat Wymore, (movie star in 1950's), was born in Salina and her parents were Jim and Minnie Wymore. Minnie told my dad that she would check in with me from time to time and would call me at the school and ask me to come over on weekends.

We became close friends and the Wymore Motel became my home away from home on weekends I needed some parenting. One day she called and ask me to come over that following Saturday. When I got there, I was walking into her part of the motel where they lived and noticed a woman working in the flower garden. Minnie called the woman inside and introduced her to me as Pat Wymore. Was I ever star struck. It was a fun weekend. We later went to a party at the motel that was for Pat and her husband Errol Flynn. He was a movie star who played the part of Robin Hood (the movie I remember) and later was an activist for Fidel Castro (Cuban dictator). I only remember him driving his yellow convertible.

Needless to say I enjoyed my time at St Johns, am sorry it closed and I credit them for turning my life around. I have always said that if I had sons, I would send them there for their education because I feel they make men out of boys and the education was top notch. You got small classrooms and outside tutoring if needed. I actually had some outside tutoring to get caught up with my classes. Every evening after dinner, I would go to Dale Browning's room and spend couple of hours doing outside work. Dale later became the President of St. Johns.

There are three types of kids that go to military and/or private schools. (1) those whose parents are rich and don't have time for their children, so the school becomes a babysitter for 9 months, (2) Those who need to go because they were discipline problems and their parents felt the school would fix them – (ME)…., and (3) those who send their kids because they feel they get a better education. I was in 2 of those categories. Need to close this part out.

I've previously written about the way I got to college, but I'll touch on it here. I took my GED to complete high school and also took a GED for equivalent to 2 years college to qualify to take the OCS exam but that also got me into college. I started college while stationed at Tinker AFB Oklahoma, going to Oklahoma City University night school and later at Baylor after the Air Force transferred me to HQ. Twelfth Air Force, Waco, Texas. Again, I went to night school. After

I was discharged I moved back home and started full time at Friends University and went there for 3 years. We had semesters back then, (three a year) and twelve to fourteen hours was full time. I tried to take that many every semester and that qualified me as full time. I also went to Wichita University, (before it became Wichita State University), one semester and then went back to Friends because I thought Wichita University was too big. I was working at Boeing on second shift and Safeway during the day as well as going to school during the day. I worked seven days a week. This was my life year around for three years.

Boeing transferred me to New Orleans on the Saturn Program and I started LSU New Orleans. From there I went to Seattle and went to Shoreline to pick up Washington credits and took off campus University of Washington night classes. I was able to start getting veteran benefits after my New Orleans assignment and when I was in Seattle area I was able to use them for school. But I could also take other classes from technical schools and I went to Ron Bailey's School of Broadcasting to help me get rid of my Kansas accent and so I could do speaking in front of groups at Boeing. Incidentally, the Bailey family ended up in prison for misappropriating funds at the school. Always something.......I did enjoy school.......

Marriage — Bigger surprise to me than to you.

**Barbara and Bob's Wedding Picture
Taken after Air Force Boot Camp**

I have always felt that marriage is forever. I don't think statistics reflect that today, but I grew up thinking that way. To do that, you have to have a certain set of values and you have to be surrounded by good healthy marriages. I was lucky in both departments.

My parents were married for all of my life. You can imagine how hurt I was when I found out my mother was married before. No kids as a result, but it still hurt. It wasn't until my dad died that I found out she was married early in her life. She was only married for six months and the divorce was because she was abused. I don't even know his name and only found out when dad died and I took her to Social Security for her benefits. In my immediate family (aunts, uncles, grandparents) on both sides, I can only think of a couple that were divorced and remarried in their lives. One of my moms brothers was divorced and remarried and only a couple of cousins were divorced and remarried. Needless to say, my dads sister adopted two girls (twins) that were both divorced and remarried. That was about it.

Of course, we all remember Frankie Purington, my second cousin whom I met when she was sixty five. She was in the entertainment business during her life and actually retired from that business. She was married and divorced three different times and until she died, she celebrated all three anniversaries.

When I started dating, I always respected the girls and later respected the women I dated. An example of that is that I had started playing around with cigarettes somewhere around the seventh grade. Nothing big, but I was huffing and puffing like all the kids I ran with. Well, I never (and I mean never) smoked around girls. In fact, I don't remember smoking around Barbara until after we were married. And I'm sorry to say, I probably was the one that got her started smoking.

I'm not going to go into the girls I dated. Needless to say, I was a late bloomer and really didn't date too many different girls but that's with my calculation. At least not serious. We all just ran around together and I guess that sufficed for some category of a date.

As I said earlier, I did meet Barbara in the summer between my eighth and ninth grades. We actually dated and went together for a couple of weeks when I was in the ninth grade. We dated all through high school, but she did break up with me after a couple of weeks of going steady. Guess I was a real "keeper". That was the only time I ever went "steady" in my life. We called it that. When we went steady, that meant we didn't date anyone else. So, you went steady until you found someone better, hmmm….wonder who he was.

This is the surprise to me. Barbara got pregnant and then we got married. No, that wasn't the surprise, **the surprise is that Barbara and I never told anyone** (at least we never discussed it with each other) and now all of a sudden when I'm 69 years old, **I find out everyone knew.** I don't know who had the big mouth (and I guess I don't want to know at this time), but no one ever let me know.

The girls and Darbie and I were in the family room just talking and I decided to take that time to tell the girls about Barbara becoming pregnant and us bringing a cute little bundle into the world. Donna sat over on the couch, and with a sheepish grin on her face, slid her hand up in the air and waved at everyone and said (Me). It was a funny moment, but a complete surprise to me that anyone knew.

Can you imagine being married at 17 years, 9 months old. In those days a man's role in the family was one of being the provider as most women didn't work, and you had to look ahead for some type of a future. Thinking about it in today's world, you would look at this situation as "hopeless". We didn't have welfare back then, and the salaries weren't very much, especially for someone that age with no experience and it certainly wasn't enough to live on. That became the reason I joined the service. I needed four more years to grow up. Best decision I ever made, except marrying Barbara.

Love is always thinking of the other person, and not thinking of yourself. Love is not selfish and Love is understanding. I always tried to believe that marriage (a product of Love) is a 60/40 relationship. If I give 60% and only expect 40% in return and my spouse does the same thing, just think of how happy we both would be. The 20% overlap would be pure bliss. This is the way I tried to be. Maybe I didn't always accomplish it, but I at least tried.

Just so everyone knows how it really was, I am going to tell the story of Barbara and I getting married. I don't want anyone out there making up bits and pieces to suit themselves. Barbara and I started serious dating between ninth and tenth grades. We actually went steady earlier but weren't ready to get as involved as "steady". Don't remember why, maybe because she thought we were too young to be going steady. After that we remained good friends. I was at their house all the time because I ran around with her brother Kenny.

After we broke up, Barbara and I had started dating others, and for a while, not each other. Even though she broke up with me, we were still REAL GOOD friends. I had been dating a girl named Marla Bracken and Barbara had gone "steady" or dating a boy named Gary. But, we would meet after our dates and then we would go out to get a hamburger at Kings X, or some soda shop (that's a drug store – like Walgreen's except they had a soda fountain) and we would just be together. Later, I went to St. Johns Military School (another story) in Salina, Kansas and we would write letters to each other. When I would come home, we would go to the show, Kings X, or somewhere we wanted to. We were in love, probably puppy love, but love to us.

When she got pregnant, there was no discussion of "abortion", (mainly because people didn't do that back then), and there was no discussion of adopting out. We thought we loved each other and that the pregnancy was the result of two people being in love, even though we were so young. That was our baby. So, the only discussion was "when were we going to get married"? Barbara was the first girl

I had sex with and I'm sure I was her first. There was none of this playing around back then like there seems to be now.

When we got married, I was 17 years, 9 months and she was 16 years 5 months old. Now think where you all were when you were 16 or 17. Actually, I don't remember our actual wedding date as we made up our date as being August 20. I think that's somewhere around Rex and my mom's birthdays. Anyway, the 20th is when we always celebrated it. As far as the marriage, we were married in Newkirk, Oklahoma. Our parents wanted us to be married out of state., that's the way they thought about it back then. We were married in front of a judge and both my dad (Parky) and Barbara's dad (Bill) were present. No, not because they thought I would run out, again that's the way people did it back then. Contrary to the thinking, "there was no shotgun present".

Because I was married I had to quit school and that's when I joined the service. After "boot camp" we were posted at Bunker Hill Air Force Base, Peru, Indiana. We had a couple of suitcases and an Air force duffel bag and rode the train for 24 hours to get there. We didn't even own a car. That was all of the possessions we had to start our marriage. Needless to say, we had a beautiful baby girl and that made us grow up fast. So I guess that Donna is to be credited for making me grow up. Don't tell her that. We were married for twenty two years before Barbara passed away. I don't know if it was a perfect marriage but we thought so. In fact, it probably wasn't, but we worked at it and stayed together until her death. I'm sure I wasn't the easiest of husbands or father, but I think we were pretty good as a couple.

I don't know if Barbara and I would have remained married if she hadn't had cancer. I do know that her illness brought us closer together. I also know a person who has a fatal illness (I think something around 85%) end in divorce. It's supposed to be hard for marriages that started out like ours to stay married, but we beat those odds. It's terrible to say that "if she hadn't had cancer", but a marriage is something you have to work at and having a disease like that just adds to the problems that already exists in a marriage. The cancer thing made us look to each other more and spend our time thinking about ourselves. We were just coming into the "empty nest" syndrome section of our marriage and we were adjusting to that. Barbara had been promoted to higher positions at Boeing and was slated to go even higher. I don't think that would have made any difference, but it might have gotten in the way. During our discussions we always came back to what we had and where we were and that's probably what kept us together. I still believe our marriage was a good one and we loved each other.

Everyone knows I had a bad marriage after Barbara, and I'm not going into that. It was not a good time in my life and I think I made enemies I still have today. I'm sure it didn't help the relationship between me and my kids and I think some resentment still remains. But if you look at that marriage, one that I shouldn't have even been in, you will see I tried. I was married for eleven years and I guess that means I don't give up easy. In the end, I did make it right but I'm still paying. I think I'm a better person today, maybe as a result of that marriage. She did have a couple of great kids and I have missed them.

Also as you know, I did meet someone who is the highlight of my life. Darbie and I have been married over 28 years now. I hope all of you have a marriage like the one I have with her. We are very respectful of each other and not demanding. We like our space, but we make time for each other. Every Friday is our date day. We don't plan any activities for ourselves with others that fall on Friday. I don't think I have even played golf on Friday except for maybe a couple of times. I always ask her permission if I think I have to do something else and it was to interfere with our Fridays and she does the same. After a person retires there seems to be more time to dote on each other. Not bragging, but we have never had an argument. That's not to say we never have disagreed with each other, but we actually discuss the issue and come to a solution. We have never gone to bed mad at each other. We always say I love you when getting into bed.

I believe you have to work at marriage and it's supposed to be forever. I didn't grow up knowing many people that had divorced parents or single parents. I think the average today for all marriages is around fifty-five percent end in divorce. Sad Percentages......

Bob and Darbie married 1-4-92 in Midwest City, Oklahoma.

(Actually the Church was in Del City, Okla)

I was really proud when Darbie's mother, (Edna) told Darbie, when she met my girls at our wedding, she saw the love my three daughters had for me and told Darbie she would be in a loving family. Anyway, I think I have been blessed in two of my marriages.

I think Darbie and I had a story-book courtship and marriage. When we met, I was working for Boeing and the Boeing workers at Tinker AFB, Oklahoma reported to me. Darbie was an executive secretary for a person who was my counterpart. So we talked some on the phone prior to my calls with her boss. We knew each other for more than two years before we started dating. The government has a straight-arrow policy where contractors can't do certain things like co-mingle. I never went to affairs the government employees went to, i.e., officer club, on-base dances, dinners etc.

After a couple of years I did start getting invited to certain events and I started attending the scheduled ones. Darbie was always there. Hence I asked her out. Went to the County Line Steak House. I remember I ordered Brisket and she ordered sauteed mushrooms. I remember offering her a bite and she took it. Later, I saw her fork coming across the table to get another bite. I told her that if she wants some she should order her own. I think she loved that so much she continued going out with me.

Picture in early days of our marriage.

Cute Couple

Since I wasn't sure if we could legally date or not, I went to my Contracts department and ask and they referred it to the company lawyers. Everyone in her organization knew she was dating someone, but they didn't know who. We couldn't tell anyone because we didn't know if it was legal. But I used this opportunity to have some fun. I would send flowers to be delivered to her at work and sign them as "The Orangutan" or "The Gorilla" or something. She would have them on her desk and all the employees would try to find out who they were from. It made her life complicated. About six months later I was invited to Tinker AFB to attend a government retirement ceremony, (around twenty military and civilian personnel were retiring), and I got a call from Contracts saying it was OK to date her if her name wasn't on a contract. I immediately called Darbie and she said no. So when I flew down to that retirement ceremony

I took her to the ceremony and that night everyone knew who she was dating. The rest of the story is our current history and you girls were part of it.

Again, the girls played a big part in my life. As I said earlier, Darbie's mother said "she was OK with her marrying me when she met my daughters at the wedding and saw how much they loved me". Still makes me get teary eyed.

The marriage was truly a family event. Darbie's brother, (Stephen Davis – A Baptist Pastor), officiated, Stephen's sons John-Paul and Caleb were ushers and Stephanie, (Stephen's daughter), sang at the wedding. Both, Darbie's father, (Paul), and her brother Greg, walked her down the aisle. My girls were there and it was a nice wedding.

I played a joke by putting the letters **HELP** on the bottom of my shoes and when we got down on our knees during the service, we had over a hundred people scrambling around trying to see and started laughing. Darbie's dad said it made the ceremony. Stephen didn't know what was going on, and a singer checked his fly while singing a song. The girls knew and Shorty, (best man), knew but that was it.

To get back at me, Darbie's dad called me right after we got to our home in Snohomish and told me that the warranty was null and void after I took Darbie over the state line. His joke has lasted longer than mine.

I consider myself a very lucky man. To have had not one but two marriages that were meaningful to my life and both were successful seems to me to be unheard of in today's world where over 55% of marriages fail. **It's probably not fair to others for me to be so lucky.** But we all know a marriage has to be worked at.

Darbie asking me "why were the people laughing

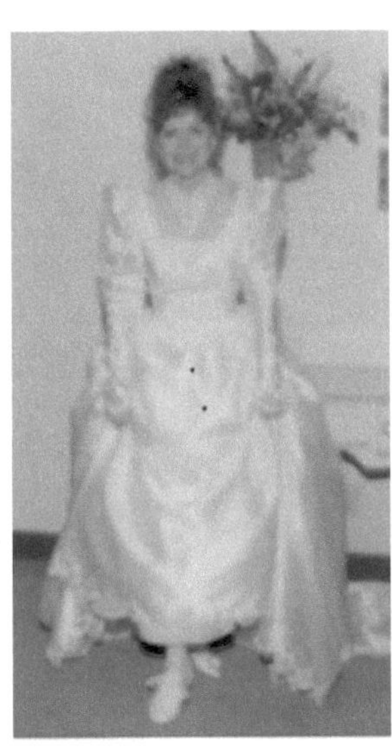

Love
these
Pictures

What is A Sister

What is a sister
  To me she's all things
She's like a butterfly…..
  who comes and goes in early spring

Being a girl…..
  she is nurturing and true
The one who keeps it together
  like putty and glue

Mine came and went
  throughout my life at times
And was so important
  I can't write in these lines

I remember comforting
  when I needed a little nudge
She never complicated issues
  and never became my judge

Now that we're older
  and ahead looms dark days
The thought of her being there
  will get me through this maze

She's still there for me
    nurturing and true
The one who keeps it together
    like putty and glue

The above poem says it all and put us together. When young, I was an older brother and Jo Ann was my younger sister. That in itself says a lot and defines our young life.

I remember walking together to and from school at a very early age. In those days we didn't get fed at school and had to come home for lunch. I would make us "egg sandwiches" every day because that's what I remember being able to cook. Just think about it, second and third graders, we were walking to and from school and I was cooking eggs. What I remember about it was I got sick of eggs. I threw up in a trash bin, (place where residents threw their trash), and hated eggs after that. It was a long time before I started eating them again.

Being an older brother and having a younger sister I'm sure we had our different paths growing up. I hope I was a good brother, but I'm not the one that decides that. The one thing we had in common is both of us felt dad was hard to get along with. Don't know if it was the times, or whether dad was raised that way or was it just me getting in his way all the time, but I think both of us felt the same way. I also think it was harder for Jo Ann because of her being a girl and probably the apple in dad's eye. He wanted to protect her. Maybe he didn't go about it the right way, but I think his motive was good.

I remember at a very early age, when I would get scared at night, I would get on my hands and knees and sneak down the hall to Jo Ann's bedroom so she could comfort me. Don't remember how often, but I do remember dad calling out "Bobby, get back to your bed" as I was sneaking.

I remember us becoming closer at different times in my life. It was probably when I needed her due to something going on in my life. After I got married, Barbara and Jo Ann became somewhat close and I remember them going places together. After her husband's death I remember her coming to New Orleans to visit us. I also remember visiting her when we went to Wichita.

There were two people in my family I always wanted to impress with my life and that was my dad and Jo Ann. Everyone else was just there.

Thanks for being in my life Jo Ann……..

Raising Kids —

"The best day in a fathers life is when his kids are born. The worst day in a fathers life is when they don't need him anymore."

This was a tough chapter to write because at the time of this writing my grandkids are raising their own kids. That means there's going to be a lot of critics out there tearing this chapter down. I hope the reader remembers the time period we were in, plus the time period our parents and grandparents were in and that's who we learned from. Workers didn't make the money they do today and there has been a lot of government intrusion into family life. We didn't have all the welfare programs that exist today and everyone was expected to take care of themselves. The government wasn't the big financial help to individuals in need, the Churches were. So, with that in mind.....

I always tell folks that if I had it to do all over again, I wouldn't teach my kids to talk until about six months prior to them starting school and I wouldn't teach them to walk until about 2 weeks before starting school. That would have made our lives a whole lot easier.

I don't really know what to tell you. As parents we're like a ruler or yard stick in life. We raised our kids as a couple and tried to put thought into what we did as far as discipline. I say, as adults, my kids would adopt the things they thought we did right, (agreed with), and throw out the ones they didn't agree with. I used to **"borry, borry, shoot the bad bear, where did we shoot him, I guess right there"** and we'd tickle them to wake them up. Borry, Borry was one of the things my kids said they'd never do to their kids. But, I think you did.

My girls always responded and minded to a finger snap when in public. If I snapped my finger, they would stop acting up or doing what they were. I know you wouldn't agree with that today because I see how kids act and what they get away with. We have a tendency to follow the model we're close to. My grandkids probably look at how they were raised and are doing the same thing with their parents. Then you get married and you have to incorporate your spouse's ideas. That's when the fun starts.

Actually, I've decided that we raise our kids by always being TOLD how to raise our kids. We're told by our parents, psychologists, teachers, friends, government, etc. You get the picture. It seems we have to appease society. We didn't have as many rules to follow because we didn't have government TELLING us how to do it. Kids nowadays can call the cops and turn the parents in for "child abuse" and suddenly your world is changed. We also think we know more than our parents and friends, and the picture just gets bigger and bigger.

Doing it all over, I would probably still discipline the same. When I think of the youth of today, I think they are very disrespectful of their parents and I have even seen that in my own family. I didn't like seeing what I did at different times, but kids are products of their parents. I believe as parents we have instilled everything in their little heads by age of five that mold them for the rest of their lives. I believe that a child's value system has been established at that point and they spend the rest of their lives living those values. As parents we don't have much time to get our job done.

We used grounding as a punishment when the kids got older. I don't think grounding helps that much, but I don't see it as being that negative either. I think grounding makes the parents lives worse and harder. We have to put up with a teenagers "looks" and "sneers" since they are home for the period of grounding. I always wondered who was punishing whom. I would say Donna was grounded most of her senior year, but of course I was joking when I said it. But she did seem to get into trouble a lot. I don't think my kids are any meaner or disrespectful to me because of how we raised them, but I think they probably made some changes in the way they raised their kids. Remember, we usually look to our parents to learn from and the way we were disciplined when we were young molded us into disciplining the way we did. So, anyone having a problem with this chapter can blame my parents and grandparents along with Barbara's parents and grandparents. Since it's not my fault, no one should be mad at me.

This is a sad story to tell, but one that helped me in my life. It only happened once (so I assume dad was not real happy about it). But it happened.

I don't remember talking back to my mom much, but I did tell her to "shut up" one time in my life. It was probably the darkest time in my childhood, bar none. Dad was a traveling salesman and left for work on Monday mornings and didn't come back until Friday evening. I always made my bed, kept my room nice and tidy and considered myself the "man of the house" while he was gone. I was fifteen and for some reason I didn't make my bed one morning when I got up and mom reminded. She again told me to make my bed a second time and I told her I didn't have time and would do it later. She told me to do it "now" and I told her to "shut up". She never said another word to me that day and we just made it through the week with short dialogue. Little did I know what "hurricane" was headed for me on Friday night when dad got home. By Friday night I was thinking I should have maybe done this before as I seemed to be getting away with it.

Well, dad walked into the house and mom immediately said "your son" told me to shut up on Tuesday morning. He didn't even take his top coat or hat off and he turned and looked at me and said "you told my wife" to shut up. In those two sentences I had lost my status as a son and all of a sudden my mom was his wife. Wow, I immediately knew something bad was going to happen. After thinking about this over the years, I think there was more than the "shut up" involved. I was the man of the house while he was gone Monday through Friday until dad came home. Then he had to establish his authority when he came home. I think this all played a role in this incident.

I was standing in the hallway and he came at me and smacked me with his hand in my face. I fell back and down and when I got up, I saw his hand coming at me again. I ducked and he hit the linen closet door behind me. I was glad that wasn't me. Now this sounds bad, but I had put myself on his level and I had no right to say what I did. I don't think I ever held it against him and other than the next morning, he never indicated he wanted to hit me like that again. And I did some pretty bad things when I was young and thought I knew it all.

I'm sure my kids will remember our evening meals. We always ate together. While that doesn't seem like much you have to remember that my sister and I never ate with our parents. We always ate by ourselves, (at least as far as I can remember). With my family I craved those evening dinners and we always took a lot of time for our discussions around the table. I have a lot of good memories coming from those dinner tables. Pam not wanting to drink the last drink from the milk carton, the mispronouncing of words (pasketti, hangleburs, etc). The last dinner table discussion I remember was when I told the girls their mother "wasn't going to come home from the hospital". That was a tough dinner for me and one I'll never forget.

Pam didn't come home one evening after school, or let me say she wasn't home when Barbara and I got home from work. I can't remember for sure, but I think there was a note on her bed. That probably was the lowest point in our lives and one of the longest nights I can remember. We called the police but they wouldn't do anything because they said a kid has to be gone for a certain amount of time before they could get involved. Most kids come back home. Anyway, after the rough night we spent, we got a call from an anonymous person the next morning around 6:30am. I will forever be indebted to him because he called. The caller said Pam was at Edmonds Community College in the cafeteria. Barbara said she couldn't go as she wasn't up to it, so their granddad and I jumped into the car and headed to school. We walked into the cafeteria and saw her sitting there. I hugged her and told her I loved her and took her home. I'm sure she was scared and the whole incident just got bigger and bigger. She was scared because she had been caught smoking at school and I guess she didn't know which was worse, home or school.

We called the school and I talked to the principal who set up a meeting with the vice principal for that afternoon. I also called the police and set up a meeting with a sergeant to have him talk to her about what happens to young girls who run away from home. When the sergeant had his discussion with Pam he wouldn't even let me in the room, so I can't expound on that. A young girl in Bellevue was killed just the week before and I think his discussion might have covered that event. After that we got Pam's hair fixed, bought her a new dress and went to school to see the vice principal. The Vice Principal told us the kids that get caught smoking had to attend a special class on Saturday morning for several hours where they were lectured and showed a movie of what smoking did to you. The principal said we didn't have to go because of the things we had done, but I wanted Pam to go and not only that but I was going to go with her. I know that embarrassed her but I sat in the class at the back of the room. Barbara and I thought parenting was all about being involved. Today, we hear too much where parents are not involved in their kids schooling and that troubles me.

When we moved to Lynnwood from New Orleans, the elementary school wanted to move Donna up a grade. I believe it was fourth to fifth. I said no, because she was changing school systems and it would be new to her and I didn't want that to be on her shoulders. We had a lot of discussions with the school administrative offices and the outcome was her being in a split class of fourth and fifth graders. I think that decision ended up being a mistake, but it was one that we allowed. Since the teacher had to split her time between the two classes, the kids had a lot of homework because of not having a teacher available all the time. I felt sorry for Donna having so much homework that I helped her do it so she could get outside and play with the rest of the kids. Her math teacher sent a note home and ask me not to help her anymore as the methods for math had changed since I was in school.

I think Donna was in junior high when she took a Spanish class and one evening she told us she was going to get a D in Spanish. I said we don't do D's in school and she told me it was a "pass or no-pass" class and wasn't important. Well, that didn't set well and I told her she had to pass or "Big Trouble" was in the wind. She got her act together, passed the class and became a teacher's aid for the rest of the year. I knew she could do it.

I'm sure that the readers have stories where you feel we, (I), screwed up in the raising department. Sometimes, I think there is still some resentment because of decisions I (or we) made. I can't put my fingers on them, but I feel that sometimes when different topics come up. Don't ask me about it, because I probably won't be able to give examples. It's always easy, as a kid, to blame our parents rather than seeing that things could have been different if we had only done it different. I can't believe how smart my parents became in just the four years I was in the Air Force. Boy did they wise up. As I grew older, I also started seeing things different.

I think Teri must have traveled through her childhood off the radar. She saw what was happening to her sisters and said to herself "I'm not going to rock the boat". She learned from the other two. When her sisters left home I ask Teri which bedroom she wanted now that it was just her at home. Her answer "I want this one and that one", (One upstairs and one downstairs). She grew up in the shadow of her sisters but when she grew up, she was the one that seemed to take up for her sisters. When pets were handed out, Donna grabbed the dog, Pam grabbed the rabbit, and Teri had nothing. Cute. I got a parakeet for Teri,(named George), and soon found out Teri was scared of birds. That didn't work out. I always thought Teri was the level headed one of the girls. Donna was first born and seems to have "first born" attributes, and Pam has middle child syndrome. Well, Teri always thought she was an "only child" and we hired the other two to play with her.

Picture the girls had professionally made for me. Love this picture.

We do have fun together

These young women are a good way to end this chapter…

These are two of my favorite pictures of my girls. I see them often and the memories they bring back are too numerous to mention. However, I see them all the time in my head. Love those girls.

Politics —

We weren't much into politics when we grew up. At least I wasn't. I was a Democrat like most everyone else and the reason was simple, because my parents were. You see, we grew up thinking the Democratic Party did a lot of good for the working class. Unions, big supporters of the Democratic Party, helped the working class by negotiating better work hours, medical, and better pay. We just sort of followed the party line. I believe unions have outlived their usefulness and because of their power, are now a roadblock. The last Democrat I voted for was John Kennedy and I wouldn't vote for him today, but I know a lot more about politics today than I did back then.

Grandma and Granddad Baker were both registered voters, but were registered in different parties. Grandma was registered a Democrat and Granddad was registered a Republican. Grandma had been associated with school and Granddad was in Business. He felt the Republicans represented the business world more than Democrats did. Both were hard line party followers. It was humorous when elections came around because they didn't speak to each other for several weeks prior to the election and several weeks following the election. Politics was serious business with them. Granddad was voted into the city council and later became a judge. He was a businessman involved in politics in a small town and he did this with only a fourth grade education. What a man. He ran and was elected as a Republican. Being in business for himself helped him understand what was happening politically long before I did. Hmmmm...wonder who Grandma voted for in that election?

In the "old" days of politics, personal and private events that happened in politicians lives were kept from the public. Lobbyists and unions were behind early politicians and everyone had their agenda. It was the goal of all lobbyists, unions, and politicians to take care of themselves first, and us voters second. Still is that way today, even more so. We are finding out about all the behind scenes activities today and I personally don't think it's pretty. We have made politicians out to be celebrities in todays world. Available media today makes it possible for them to be in the limelight, almost on a daily basis. President John Kennedy was the first President to bring the media into the forefront, it was called television. The bottom line is that Politicians are people just like us, and they're supposed to "represent" us.

In my early years we looked up to politicians and listened to every word they said with bated breath. We took them at their word. Today, we listen to every word with bated breath, but we're learning to look "behind" the words. This is true of both parties. Most politicians have one thing they look out for, i.e., themselves, and those who do are self-serving.

Jack Kennedy was the first President I paid attention to. I look at him today through the eyes of his accomplishments. It was actually Joe Kennedy, his dad, who got him elected with a deal he made with the unions. It had been Joe Kennedy, the father, who wanted his oldest son (Joseph P. Kennedy, jr) to be the son who ran for President. After he died at the young age of twenty nine, Jack Kennedy became the heir apparent. It was also Joe Kennedy who "required" Bobby Kennedy be Jack's Attorney General and this was because Joe wanted someone in the family to have Jack's back. It became known later that Bobby actually made most of the decisions of the White House and he probably should have been the one that was President. Jack never wanted to be President; he just wanted to be a History Teacher at Harvard. We didn't know all of this Kennedy history back then.

We also didn't know about Jack's affairs back then. It was probably rumored, but wasn't out in the public like those kinds of incidents today. It wasn't until Bill Clinton ran for President and the press caught wind of his affairs while governor of Arkansas, that the press started going public with the scandals and this was the beginning of today's method of covering a candidate. It was a Sixty Minutes TV show where Bill and Hillary Clinton appeared to confirm the stories and apologize to the public. This has gravitated to Soundbites. This type of Journalism has now translated to all candidates, even in local elections. Currently the press seems to find more dirt on Republicans than they do Democrats. Or they just gloss over any Democrat dirt. There were spotted incidents, like Senator Gary Hart being caught boating with someone other than his wife, but these incidents were few. Now, the press digs up dirt and they figure its fair game. It has to do with ratings.

In the past you never knew for sure which party a journalist was registered as while they were reporting. They told both sides of the headlines. Take Walter Cronkite as an example. One of the best journalists we've ever had. We didn't know he was a registered member of the Democratic party, far left wing democrat at that, until after he retired. Where does that leave us today. We have to be smart enough to recognize all politicians and journalists have their own agenda and to make important voting decisions requires us to read everything we can to get to the heart of a candidate's platform.

When we went to school K through 12, we didn't get influenced by our teachers. Maybe because we couldn't vote yet. Now these so called "Educators" feel they have to influence their students and teach "their" version of politics, which by the way is democrat. Teachers unions dominate their profession and unions favor democrats. The curriculum has changed so much and today's students don't get the advantage of some of the world history we had. What is being taught and studied is not accurate. History may have negative periods of time, but it is history and should help in molding ones mind and a nations path. Today's college is worse than our K through 12 influence.

It can get confusing. In today's world, it's not enough to be a Democrat or Republican. You have to be Moderate Democrat, left or right wing, Fiscal Democrat, or Tea Party Republican. The Independent party joins with Democrats when voting in congress and the Libertarian party usually joins with Republicans. A good example of wrangling going on today is what's going on within the Democratic party. Far left Democrats are attempting to rob their party from a more moderate party line and there is also an influx of Socialists attempting to steal the Democratic platform. If successful, the result will be financially devastating to our country. Again, we have to look behind the sound bites from journalists.

We're seeing youngsters starting to become involved in politics and some of their ideas are starting to make me nervous. It appears to me these youngsters haven't paid attention to the same history we grew up with. Yes, I'm talking about the Socialists party. It boggles my mind that anyone in the USA would even exercise the thought of being a Socialist when we have the history of socialism in the world and the impact on people living under that system. Just talk to someone who lived under their leadership.

President Bill Clinton was actually impeached in the House of Representatives, but not one Democrat Senator voted to impeach him in the Senate. Most people think he was impeached for the Lewinsky oral sex activity in the White House. Not true, he was impeached for lying under oath and lying to the public. Both were very serious offenses.

Younger generations have witnessed two impeachments in their lifetime, President Bill Clinton and now President Donald Trump. Articles of Impeachment were brought against President Trump in the House of Representatives for abuse of power and obstruction of congress. Again, the Senate acquitted Trump of these charges in February 2020. With Bill Clinton, sex was the reason he felt he needed to lie about the incident. With President Trump, the Democratic House took almost three years to come up with something to charge him with. When you compare the two, the latter was truly a political show. When I watched the actions of the House and Senate activities, I could not see why the Democrats didn't rebel against their party for the sham. Guess that's politics.

Leading up to my voting, I look to a candidates platform in determining who I'm going to vote for. I watch all debates during the primaries and afterwards when they become candidates, to look in depth as to each politician's platform and their voting record. After I pick the platform I feel comfortable supporting, it becomes evident where my party support lies. Both political parties look at the same platform items, however their approach to those items are different. These items are; freedom of speech, 2nd amendment, made in America, fossil fuel, climate control, transparency, business regulations, taxes, abortion, terrorism, and Foreign Affairs. I didn't put these items in any specific order.

I'm not trying to give anyone a civics course, but this is how I learned politics. Politics should be an ongoing learning activity for everyone and you should be able to change if something no longer agrees with your way of thinking. Anyway, I'm not going to try to make anyone think my way, but I would like everyone to study politics more than what's in the press and look behind the politicians and those professors in school.

Just Plain Fun Stuff —

This is where I really get to take a look back in time at memories. So many are etched in my mind surrounding our early family and growing up years. It's hard to pinpoint where to start. Just start with the little kids, I guess.

I'm apologizing for using Donna so much in this story. But, after all, she was the first born and as I said earlier we didn't take "child raising" in school and therefore had to learn child raising using her as the example. Hence, Donna became our school for learning. We were training her and she was training us. As we moved through our lives, she proved to be the best example we could have had.

Having Donna was the first happy fun time I remember. Don't get me wrong. This wasn't the first happy time, but as our family it was. Nothing like having a baby in the house to bring smiles on your face. Her name originated from us wanting to name her "Dawn", but couldn't figure out a way to make it sound good with a middle name. We wanted "Lynn" for a middle name, after Becky Lynn Vanderhoofven – Barbara's cousin, and just couldn't get it to work. So, Dawn became Donna. It worked for us. Sorry Donna, if you like Dawn better.

Donna started standing in the palm of my hand at 3 months.

She was such a happy baby and having her with us just made us happy all the time. She weighed eight pounds, two ounces and in those days, if the baby was over eight pounds at birth, they started them out with whole milk instead of formula. Of course we couldn't afford a pot to pee in and not having to buy formula was OK with us.

I don't think the word "babysitter" was invented yet. We wouldn't go anywhere to visit where my kids weren't also invited. That was the rule in the Baker household. Since we couldn't or wouldn't go anywhere without her, we ended up with friends who also had kids they wouldn't or couldn't go anywhere without. So, we did family things like going over to someone's house and playing cards, games, or going to parks and beaches. You know things that were free. So the fun time was with good friends who were in the same boat as us. I spoke earlier of our "International" friends, and that's when we met them.

I attribute Donna as being the one that got me back with my relatives in Leavenworth. I had talked earlier of a rift between mom's brothers and sisters regarding their mother. As families no one was talking to each other. I had continued a relationship with Mary Lou, mom's sister, and was talking to her about my upcoming transfer to

Oklahoma City. She wanted us to drive through Leavenworth. So we did and I was reunited with Aunt Dorothy and Uncle Burton. Probably because of Donna and the fact that Burton just got their adopted girl, Judy, we were invited to stay in Leavenworth for a couple of days. That way, we could compare kids.

We never had a crib for Donna until she was around fifteen months old and she actually slept in a drawer in our bedroom for most of that time. We purchased a car bed from Sears to make the trip to Oklahoma City. Sears didn't have the size we ordered and sent the next larger size, so she graduated from the drawer to the car bed. A car bed had a couple of hooks that fit over the back of the front seats and a base that could be either back seat height or floor height. Needless to say she was very good in both of her beds, unlike Lacy, Donna's youngest daughter, who would "dive" out of her crib, landing on her head.

Donna was a couple of years old before Pamela came along. Pamela Jo (Pam) was named after my sister Jo Ann. Pam just made things more fun. However the fun became something different. We now had two kids to bounce around. Again, we had a lot of local fun stuff to do. I was working two jobs by now and my time was starting to be a little more limited. The fun stuff was me playing with the girls and just being home. We spent many a Sunday at Lake Waco, as it was free and free was good. I would wake up the girls in the middle of the night so I could watch them find their Easter eggs before I went to work. It seemed to work out that we always took inventory on Easter day at the grocery store. I had to get the girls up a little earlier.

After I got out of the service, I still had two jobs; in fact I had two jobs for 3 more years. I was starting college in Wichita, Kansas, at Friends University and two jobs and college **really** limited my time. I remember getting home from Boeing around 1:15am after 2nd shift and Barbara would have two sandwiches and a glass of milk ready for me. This would have been my 4th meal of the day. I Only weighed

139 pounds back then. Love to be there today. Anyway, Donna always seemed to be up for whatever reason (I know I woke her up sometimes) and she would get to come out for 15 minutes or so and that was a fun time. At least for me. Maybe that's why today she likes to sleep in. Don't know if that has any bearing or not.

Teresa Sue (Teri) was born when I got out of the service. Barbara was pregnant when I was discharged and the government wouldn't pay for the medical bills. I went to work at Boeing and in those days you had to have your insurance for nine months BEFORE they would pay for a child to be born. Now, people are griping because the government want's insurance to cover birth control pills. I remember the payoff for the hospital was around $320.00. We had to pay both the hospital and doctor ($125.00) BEFORE her birth. I have always wondered what the hospital and doctor would have done if "I hadn't" paid off the bill before her birth. I guess today they would have some government program that would take care of it.

Everyone would ask who Teri was named after and Barbara came up with "one of Bob's old girlfriends". I don't remember ever having a girlfriend named Sue, but it sounded good. Barbara didn't want two kids in diapers at the same time so she worked real hard to get Pam potty trained "before" Teri was born. Sure made our lives easier as back then they didn't have pampers. Everyone used linen diapers and you washed every couple of days. Pam was potty trained around fourteen months. Boy that was a help.

Having all three of the girls and no money meant we needed to do things that were cheap. That's probably why we did a lot of traveling to relatives homes. Since I worked two jobs and went to college year around, I didn't have much time off. Certainly not like today when you get a month off and all that sick leave you can use. I only had the two weeks off in between semesters at college. So, we went places that were close which resulted in going to grandparents, uncles and aunts and friends. I can remember one time getting off at my usual

1:00 am shift at Boeing, hurrying home, packing the car real quick and leaving about 2:00 am heading for New Orleans. In those days we knew there were motels, but no one slept in one. At least not in my crowd. Why do that when you can sleep in the car or drive all night. Now you think in terms of paying $100.00 + just to get a room in a motel around 5:00pm in the evening. Glad I can afford a room at this time in my life.

That same trip we were south of Alexandria and everyone in the car was asleep. We had a Chevy II Nova station wagon back then. Lots of room to sleep. Anyway, I was getting tired and everyone was asleep, so I pulled over in a rest stop to catch a few moments. Well, I was dead asleep and a cow put its head in the driver's side window, licked my face and moo'd. It sure scared the crap out of all of us. Woke me up and I didn't have any more problems staying awake. I drove on to New Orleans and we stayed with Barbara's folks Tillie and Bill. Also saw Leonard and Helen during the same trip. I think Ken and Rex came in from Seattle, Washington area during that trip and it was fun to see them. Good times.

We spent a lot of time with Shorty and Arlynn. Arlynn was a best friend of Barbara's and Shorty was my best friend in school. Shorty decided after high school to go to work for Wyle and McCall's Shoe Store in Park Lane shopping center. He was doing this while I was working and going to college. He had more money than I did and paid for most of whatever we did. Now that's a friend. We normally got together on Saturday nights and played cards, drank beer and just had fun. Reason for Saturday nights was that my hours on Saturday at Safeway were from 9:00 am to 5:00 pm and I didn't go to work until Sunday at 12:00 pm to 9:00 pm. That way, Saturday night was my weekend.

Shorty later married Joyce who has become an important part of our lives and we currently get together and take vacations. We visit each other's homes as often as we can playing games, reminiscing, and telling lies about the past. We've gone to vacation spots, rode in helicopters, and just do what old people do. Love our lives today. Shorty was one of the best friends anyone could have. Never judgmental and always upbeat. He helped me keep my head on. Love that guy..

Only went drinking with my dad one time in my life. He and I didn't seem to get along all that well, I spoke of it earlier, and we just seemed to rub each other wrong. He did let me drive his car on vacation one time, because his car had air conditioning. In fact it was when he brought his car over to give to me that we went drinking together. Like I said it was the first time. We told jokes, laughed and had one of the best times of my adult youth. Little did I know that in a few years, he would soon be gone from my life? Both good time and sad…..

I had a 1959 Ford at the time of my vacation, with no air conditioning. I talked about it earlier. It had been a police car and as a result it was fast. Dad borrowed that car from me when I drove his on vacation. When I got home from the trip, it was late in the day and I hadn't had time to clean up the car when dad called and said he was coming to pick his car up. I told him I wanted to clean it up and he said he would take care of that by taking it to a car wash. I didn't know the rest of the story for about 3 months. Mom told me the story….. It seems dad was on Kellogg street sitting at a stop light and this guy came up alongside him and both revved up their engines and when the light changed both took off. Mom said dad got up to 80 MPH when the cop stopped him. Mom said the cop called him a "middle aged delinquent" and basically made him feel like a criminal. Hence, he wanted his car back. He never told me that story.

Christmas wasn't big for me when I was young. I got presents, but don't remember being all excited about Christmas morning and playing with toys. I think it was because for the most part I got clothes. We probably always needed clothes in those days. I did get a bicycle once and I remember a pair of pistol holsters that were hand made by an Indian in Oklahoma. I also got a Lionel Train Set and I don't know where they ended up. I remember spending hours playing with that train set. Wish I had it today. The bicycle was a Western Flyer. I remember the first thing I did to it (as soon as I could) was turn the handle bars upside down. We also put playing cards in the rear spokes so they made a clacking sound representing a motor. That was the cool thing to do. One time we got a big snow storm the week before Christmas and I didn't have gloves. Dad pointed out a present under the tree and said "wonder what's in that package"? You guessed it, "gloves". I always wondered how he knew what was in that package?

Western Flyer Bicycle

One of the neatest memories I have is when Lacy was born. Donna wanted me to be with her when she had Lacy and that meant being at the hospital and being **IN THE BIRTH ROOM**. You have to remember when all three of the girls were born, fathers were not allowed to be in the birthing room. I had to sit in the fathers waiting room until the big moment came and they would come and get me. The big moment was after the baby is cleaned up and the mother was also cleaned up. When Lacy was born, that meant **I WAS THERE** when the business happened. The doctor wanted me to be the photographer (OK with me as I was at Donna's head). Since the doctor was the director, he called all the shots. When the action happened and Lacy was coming into this world, the doctor said "come here quickly" before it's too late. It was the neatest thing I ever got to do, but I'm sure all of my son-in-laws knows what I'm talking about. Thank you Donna for that memory.

When Teri was born, the doctor, who knew I had two other girls, just looked through the window into the fathers waiting room and shrugged his shoulders. Guess that's his way of telling me I had another girl. Barbara thought she had a boy as the first thing she told me was "they already circumcised" him and I said they did a real good job. I was happy she was a girl.

Pam was my buddy. On fishing trips she would get up with me and we would fish the early hours, then we'd come back to the trailer and get everyone else up. Traveling, I would get up early (around 5am) and drive just to get some hours and miles under my belt and I would let Barbara and the girls sleep in the trailer. Pam would always get up with me and sit beside me in the car, talk to the truckers on the CB and pour me coffee. Just her and I. She says she didn't want me to fall asleep while driving. That was neat......Then we would get the call on the CB from Barbara saying "we're up, stop when you can". Pam sat in the front seat with me when I gave the girls skiing lessons on Snoqualmie. This time, however, she held a flashlight in her hands and watched me making sure I wasn't going to sleep while driving. She would flash me with the flashlight when she thought I needed it. I cherished those moments and always looked forward to the next time.

My memories of Teri are one of a kid with a good heart. She only had good things to say about everyone. Except when it came to taking up for her sisters. I remember her saying, "Don't talk to my sister that way" as she was flying by me and heading towards the front door after some neighbor girl. But the biggest heart came from her when her mother was having a difficult time with her cancer. The other girls were living away from home, Donna lived in Tacoma and Pam was working at Allstate (I believe). Teri was the one remaining at home and was a senior in High School at the time. Barbara would give her money or a check for buying groceries and running errands. Most of the time I wasn't even aware. Teri still has this kind heart and treats others with great respect.

There are so many memories I could write a book just about them. But suffice it to say that these memories are what molds a person into who they are. We become defined by these memories. And because my memories are good ones, my life has been good.

Traveling

Not going to spend much time. Think it would be boring to most readers. Girls know we've traveled a lot. Started when the kids were young. I think it's because when I got out of the service and started attending college and working at Safeway and Boeing, and the fact I went to school year around, we just had to get away to somewhere. Traveling was primarily to friends and family for the most part. But it allowed us to wind down and take it easy for a while.

I've been in all 50 states and was lucky enough to travel Europe, Saudi Arabia, Orient and places in-between. Darbie has been in all states but three. We went to Europe on a Viking River Cruise and stepped foot in seven countries. We've slept in cars (no money), motels, travel trailers, and motor homes. One year we even took a seven week trip on our motorcycle that started in Tucson, AZ, to Florida and up the east coast to Interstate 40 and back to Tucson. Great trip but wouldn't be wanting to start out today on that trip.

We lived in our motor home for six months while the contractor was building our home in SaddleBrooke.

Didn't add to Car purchases as it didn't fit the physical description.

It was a 1995 Bounder 34 foot.

Actual Boss of the Motor Home

Her name was Sissy Sue and she weighed all of 8 1/2 lbs.

When traveling Florida, we stumbled into Bernie Little's "Bud" racing boat. He would bring it to Seattle to run in the yearly Sea Fair race on Lake Washington. He's now passed on and I don't think his boat comes to Seattle anymore. We were surprised when we saw it and more surprised when we looked **at the license plate** (Washington). It's a personal tag with **KT** on it. **KT stands for K&T Machine shop** on Mukilteo Speedway, Washington. Ken did a lot of work for Bernie when he was in Seattle, plus I think some of the crew live in Seattle.

Needless to say, we have always enjoyed traveling but we're running out of time. And this pandemic thing hasn't helped any. Getting old isn't helping either. It hurts just doing something anymore. Everything aches and it almost seems like we can't be too far from the doctor. I address my "Aches and Pains" later in a chapter by that name. What does this mean? It means traveling has been minimized.

Traveling has always been a big part of the Baker Family's life. We've all enjoyed it. Our sons-in-law have not traveled as much as we have. They take vacations but they either fly or go to eastern Washington. They enjoy it.

Recently, Howard and Donna ordered a Dodge Ram Longhorn pickup and picked it up in Tucson. Howard actually ordered it and when it came in Donna and Howard flew down to pick it up. So, they had to drive it home. Howard said it was a real good trip and he couldn't believe all the things to see between Tucson, Arizona and Bothell, Washington. Now that he and Donna are retired I expect to see them drive down when they find the time. Mike and Pam have a 5th wheel and I expect to see them after he retires. Don't know about Ken and Teri, we'll just have to wait and see.

Bob And Pat's Story

It's a Small World, Isn't It

What do you think about when you hear that statement? That's right, Disney World or just plain Disneyland. But, to get to the punch line, you have to read further.

I accompanied Darbie to the theater one evening, just after I had neck surgery and was in a neck brace. The lady sitting next to me at the show has a friend, Pat Ford, who was going to have a similar surgery. The woman asked if her friend could talk to me and ask questions about my neck surgery, like who did it, how long was surgery, etc. I obliged and told the lady a little about it and that was it.

A week later that same lady came up to me and told me her friend was at the theater that night and would it be OK if she brought her friend over to talk. The friend was scheduled for her surgery that following Monday and I said sure, be happy to. This is what we do here in SaddleBrooke. Tell each other who are doctors are, etc.

So, Pat Ford and I discussed the surgery and all the following complications that come with it. Incidentally, she even had the same surgeon I had. When the discussion about the surgery ended, the questions started. While all discussions about medical procedures and geography usually represent about 90% of conversations in SaddleBrooke, they do eventually gravitate to how long have you lived in SaddleBrooke and where did you come from. I told Pat that "We're in our nineteenth year at SaddleBrooke and I'm from Wichita, Kansas" originally. Pat responded with "My husband Bill and I are in our fifteenth year and I'm from Kansas also, but from a small town you probably never heard of". I said "try me." Pat answered "Beloit." I immediately said, "My grandparents lived in Beloit, Kansas." (Beloit is a small town with about 4500 residents, mostly farmers.) Pat asked "Who are they" and I said "Roy and Kitty Baker." Pat said, "I know Roy and Kitty". Roy had a barbershop in town. Then she said her maiden name was "Hill" and I responded "I knew a Hill, Frank Hill." Pat said, "That's my Grandfather," and the conversation eventually wandered in the direction of "Harold Hill" who I said was my dad's cousin who would pick me up at the bus station when I went to town to take care of Grandma Kitty. Pat said, "Harold is my father and we're the only Hills in Beloit as Harold was an only child." It turned out that Pat's grandmother and Bob's grandfather are brother and sister. Guess what? Pat and I are related. Actually, we're second cousins. Needless to say at the time of the article I wrote for the SaddleBrooke paper, our friendship was only a month or so old, but it goes back well over 65 years. We even knew some of the same people growing up.....

**It's a Small World, Isn't it.....
especially in SaddleBrooke!**

NEWS FLASH!!!!!!

Since I met and wrote the above, I have another 2nd cousin now living in SaddleBrooke. In fact he lives about two blocks away from us and his last name is "Bowen". Sound familiar? Actually, Jeff Bowen was adopted and his adopted father is the Bowen. Jeff and his wife Els have now lived here for the past couple of years. We haven't run genealogy or tried tracing to find out for sure but timing and ancestry seem to bear out that it "could be"…... We're having fun with it, so why ruin a fun thing. He is the master of the "one liners". We do normal SaddleBrooke things like going out to eat, play golf and tell lies. Works for us.

Getting Old is Not For Sissies (Nam be-Pam be)

When young, you have your toys. Well, that doesn't change just because you're older. When old age starts creeping in, you still have toys, but the toys change.

When young you have your little cars, dolls, dress up clothes, cowboy outfits, children books, bicycles, and other toys, etc. You get the picture...... Now we still have toys, but they're different. We now have Blood Pressure machines, oxygen tanks, wheelchairs (instead of toy cars) all kinds of aids to help us get through the day. We have all kinds of knee problems (right knee, left knee and "weenie"). We have braces for knees, elbows, feet, ankles shoulders and everything else that needs a little help.

You probably won't remember, when young and you had a trike and ran into everything and finally, your mom and dad say "Take that thing outside". Well, it's the same when you get old. Except it has more consequences, i.e., you're in a car and it drifts, you seem to get too close to the car in front, or, you don't seem to watch your speed very close. Well, they now have cars to help in that arena and we happen to have one. Our car (with adaptive cruise on) now senses when I'm too close to the car in front, let's me know (alarm) when

I have a potential problem coming and lets me know when I drift. What a deal, all I have to do is remember to set the cruise. Every ole fart ought to own one of these.

I found a way to travel on trips that seem to help make it safe for us to be on the highways. I put a sign in the back window's that say in bold letters **"This driver is over 80 years old, stay away"**. You can't imagine the quick movements other drivers make to get at least one lane away from us. Works for me.

Everything is different today. Never in my wildest thinking would I have believed old age is like it is. I find things every day that I now do different or have to figure out some other way of doing it. Like working in the yard. I used to just plop down on the lawn and do my work either in the flower bed or other areas. I now have to look for something to hold on to that will hold my weight so I can contort my body and gradually scoot down to my knees. That's just the beginner, I now have to worry whether or not I can actually get back up.

When first asked "how're you doing today"? I would answer "Great, It's a great day in SaddleBrooke". Now when ask, I say **"I drink my moo and do my poo, that's all I do"**. I think they get the message.

I get scared I'm going to start smelling old. By that I mean the smell that is evident when going to a nursing home to see the residents. My guess is it comes from bodily functions that seem to be leaking and all the medicines in the facility. I've even seen it on our golf course and different functions we've had in the ballrooms and meeting rooms. There's a whole lot of flatulence going on here in SaddleBrooke. I read recently that New Zealand is going to tax farmers in an attempt to curb cow flatulence. Maybe they'll figure they need to tax retirement communities for the same reason.

When couples have babies today, there are diapers available to them with names like "pampers", "Luvs", and "Huggies", which are cutie names. Now that we're older, our diapers are called "depends". That's not fair.

I had a doctor once tell me that he was going to prescribe 25 Mg's of Viagra for me. I asked him what 25 Mg's would do for my sex (they sell Viagra in minimum of 50 mg tablets). He politely said "nothing", however it will keep me from peeing on my feet.

The other day I was walking behind 3 guys while going into the clubhouse and they were talking. The first guy said "Sure was Windy today. The second guy said "Thought today was Thursday". And the third guy said "I'm Thirsty too, lets get a drink when we go into the Clubhouse". This place is a cash cow for hearing aids, and most end up on our dresser because we forget where we placed them.

Virtual doctor appointments seem to be the new normal. I hate those words" New Normal". It comes with actions that seem to be the new way we're going to have to live. We're not techies and everyday we are being forced to agree to something we're not comfortable with and virtual appointments are one that I don't like. Maybe that's because my Proctologist wanted me to have a virtual appointment and I decided "I think not" and told him I was going to have to come in. No computer exam for me.

The one thing I want to leave you with is that I wasn't prepared for being "old". I don't mean anything negative about it, but it just got here faster than I expected. I think for me it started around 78 years old. From there on now things just seem to be happening in leaps and bounds. Guess this time is the twilight of ones life.

I'm not ready to turn the light out yet.

Aches and Pains

This is the worst chapter in the whole book. This is where I bring up medical issues. Even though it's not a fun item to talk about, it's something that's important to immediate family members. I wish I had known about the medical issues of my mom and dad. I do know they died of heart complications. Going back from there would be nice but not readily available. While older generations did have some of the diseases we do today, they just died. They probably had cancers, diabetes etc., however, in those days they just died of old age.

Our generations are the lucky ones, because of our better medical knowledge today we get to know what our medical issues are, and we also will be able to know what we will die from. OK, now to me.

Growing up I was just like kids of today. I was invincible. During my teen years and into my twenties I was pretty healthy. Around 28, I started having back issues. I spent a lot of time at the doctors and all they did in those days was aspirin. I took such large doses and a high quantity and my ears started ringing all the time, and I finally just threw those pills away. It wasn't until I was 55 when I took my first MRI on my back and found out that I was born with a slight case of "scoliosis". Of course I never knew I had scoliosis and now days school nurses check students backs.

Also around twenty eight years old, I started having early stages of a disease called "restless leg" syndrome, but at that time it wasn't necessary to take pills. I broke a couple of bones on the road to retirement (left elbow and left foot) but other than that I was pretty healthy. Then came retirement. I always say "I saved my money getting ready for retirement and I spend all my time in retirement taking care of my medical". This may not be true, but sometimes it seems that way.

Since retirement, I've had:

1. Two back fusion surgeries (T-9 through S-1 = 10 vertebra's).
2. One neck fusion surgery (C-3, 4, and 5 = 3 vertebra's).
3. Gall Bladder removed.
4. Thumb surgery on right arthritic thumb.
5. Right Hip Surgery – still going through problems with that.
6. Three Tia's several years ago – resulted in Carotid Artery Surgery.
7. Currently wearing a "heart monitor" embedded in my chest for up to three years checking for A-Fib. **Note:** Last year I had some double vision issues and was checked several ways to Sunday for A-Fib. Doctors said I had hundreds of Tia's in a six week period and they didn't know why or what was causing it.
8. Gout – This used to be called "A Rich Man's" disease because it's related to food, (form of arthritis) - "Uric Acid" in the blood. This can be caused from genetic factors. Pill's do control.

This list identifies a couple of areas to be concerned about. (1) Arthritis, (2) Back problems, (3) Restless Leg Syndrome, and, (4) Heart Issues. These are all diseases that have genetic implications. I don't think these are big problems, however Donna may not agree. The big things we get nervous about is Heart Issues, Big C – Cancer, and a host of other issues that cause us to spend time at doctors offices. I actually lump all the above issues into one main disease and I call it "Old Age". This disease has all the elements of all of the other diseases and even includes the current "Pandemic" we're going through.

I don't think you should get nervous about the above information, but you might be prepared to be able to talk with your doctors about my medical issues as it pertains to you.

Of course, your mother had "Hodgkin's Disease", which brought on several other complications and she actually died of "Acute Leukemia" resulting from years of chemotherapy. Hodgkin's Disease is in the Herpes Strain (cold sores, shingles, etc.) and she had a hard time with "Shingles", and was anemic during Chemotherapy. Because of taking a lot of Chemotherapy for a big portion of 12 years, her issues at the end were mostly due to resulting medical issues. Now days the cancer treatments are much easier on the body and Hodgkin's Disease is a curable cancer if caught early. I think enough said…...

Letter To My Girls

Hiddy –

Thought I'd take some time to write a note to my daughters. I've been scratching my head and wondering how to start. Actually, this whole book is a letter to you. It seems to me that it shouldn't be difficult writing to someone I've known all their lives and have loved so much. It was an instant love for me and it's hard to describe, but each one of you know what I mean because you all have your own kids.

I've only tried to do the best I could. One has to remember that when your mother and I started on this journey; (1) we were young; (2) neither of us had taken a course in school called "Child Rearing 101"; (3) we were coming into this on the ends of an earlier time in history (depression) when no one had much nor did we expect much; and, (4) we only had our parents to model from.

Now... I don't look at any of the above times in our lives as negative at all, especially when I see the young kids of today. We had **discipline** (probably seemed harsh at times), **fun** (rolling around on the floor wrestling 3 girls was the highlight of my day), preparing and getting ready for holidays and special events **(anticipation)**, and we didn't have this "keeping up with the Jones" attitude that seems to exist today. Note: Kids also minded and listened.

As a family, your mother and I always looked forward to our **family time**, (dinner time around the table was the best for me). Our vacations were probably the **second-best** time because we were always together and usually traveled to our friends and family (unfortunately for you vacations came in the summer when you girls were out of school). **Number three** was being able to watch you grow and become young ladies and the women you turned out to be today. I can't think of anything that would make me more proud than the way you ended up. Beautiful women with beautiful families and a pretty good head on your shoulders.

My hope and prayer for you is that you are able to enjoy the life you have as much as I've enjoyed mine. If you do, you will be successful. Don't take anything for granted. Be happy with what you have and the families you've brought into this world. Those are the memories you take with you.

Your Dad…...

Conclusion —

Time to go....I've taken enough of your time........

My life has been a good life. I think I handled everything that was thrown at me. I know others were involved in some of the trials and tribulations that came my way and I hope I handled them OK. If I didn't, I'm truly sorry.

Growing up I thought my childhood was bad in some respects. But a couple of things have changed that idea. One was writing this story. The other was back into the 80's when my mother moved to Seattle and I listened to her talk to my daughters about my childhood. When I listened to her tell those stories, I realized I had built a wall around my upbringing and I was steadfast in thinking, "it wasn't as good as it could have been". Those stories made me realize, "I did have a good childhood", and just maybe....... I could have been a better son.

www.ingramcontent.com/pod-product-compliance
Lightning Source LLC
Chambersburg PA
CBHW051451250726
48655CB00001B/347